Legality and Local Politics

LEE BRIDGES
Institute of Race Relations,
London
CHRIS GAME
Institute of Local Government Studies,
University of Birmingham
OWEN LOMAS
and
JEREMY McBRIDE
Faculty of Law,
University of Birmingham
STEWART RANSON
Institute of Local Government Studies,
University of Birmingham

Avebury

Aldershot · Brookfield USA · Hong Kong · Singapore · Sydney

Published by

Avebury

Gower Publishing Company Limited
Gower House
Croft Road
Aldershot
Hants GU11 3HR
England

Gower Publishing Company
Old Post Road
Brookfield
Vermont 05036
USA

British Library Cataloguing in Publication Data

Bridges, Lee
  Legality and local politics.
  1. Local government —— Great Britain ——
  State supervision
  I. Title
  344.102'42   KD4765

ISBN 0-566-05430-2 ✓

Printed and bound in Great Britain by
Biddles Limited, Guildford and King's Lynn

LEGALITY AND LOCAL POLITICS

Contents

Preface

The decision of the House of Lords in the 'Fares Fair'
case, which concerned the fares policy of the Greater
London Council (GLC) and the events which followed were of
major significance to both local government and
Administrative Law. Placed in the wider context of
increasing judicial involvement in local government
decision-making, they were therefore ideally suited to
inter-disciplinary study by administrative lawyers and
political scientists specialising in public administration
and local government. This approach enabled separate but
related concerns about the impact of judicial decisions to
be investigated from different perspectives. It also made
possible study of the inter-relationship between local
government decision-making and its attributes, and those of
the higher courts and the law.

It was these considerations which brought together the
present authors from the Institute of Local Government
Studies and the Faculty of Law at Birmingham University. A
central focus of research and teaching at the Institute has
been the changing pattern of relations between central and
local government and thus the development of increased
financial, legal and administrative controls upon local
authorities. The Faculty of Law has a longstanding
commitment, dating back to the establishment of its
Institute of Judicial Administration in 1969, to fostering
inter-disciplinary studies of law and the legal system and
their wider impact on society. Common interest and
complementary skills suggested the possibility of research
collaboration into the increasingly significant issue of
judicial intervention in local authority decision-making.
Our proposed research project 'Legal Judgments and Local
Authority Decision-Making' was supported by the Economic

and Social Research Council (ESRC) and our report forms the basis of this book.

Working together was very rewarding. We feel we learned a great deal from our investigation and hope that, at least some of this, is passed on here. We are aware, however, that our study represents a modest step in investigating and trying to make sense of the relationship between Administrative Law and Public Administration at the local level. Thus, our explanation and analysis will be developed in later papers and articles on some aspects of our study. We would, therefore, warmly welcome comments and criticisms from whatever quarter.

Writing as well as fieldwork has benefitted from both specialised and co-operative working. Particular members of the team took responsibility for drafting chapters: thus Bridges and Ranson took the lead in Chapter 2, McBride in Chapter 3, Game in Chapter 4, Lomas in Chapter 5, Lomas and McBride in Chapter 6, Ranson in Chapter 7 and Ranson, Lomas and McBride in Chapter 8.

There are many who deserve our thanks. Chief amongst them, however, are John Stewart, Professor of Local Government and Administration in the Institute of Local Government Studies, who was primarily responsible for bringing us all together, the ESRC for funding us, and the local authorities and passenger transport authorities, without whose co-operation the fieldwork would not have been possible. We would also like to thank Andrew Sanders and Kieron Walsh, as well as John Stewart, for reading and commenting on our drafts. Finally, we wish to thank all the Secretaries in the Faculty of law and in the Institute, in particular, Judy Cohen, Gillian Jones, Diana Myers and Lynne Dixon for their help in typing, re-typing, typing ... for 5 authors!

1 Introduction

Local government in this country works within a statutory
framework. In law, local councils are statutory
corporations with powers and duties given to them by Acts
of Parliament to carry out various functions. These
councils also, however, constitute an important elected
tier of local government and politics, with many of their
powers drafted in terms which permit a considerable breadth
of discretion and innovation.

There is, then, an inbuilt tension in the sphere of local
government between local political decision-making and the
law. But it is a tension that, for **most** of the past sixty
years or so, has lain comparatively dormant. Certainly,
there have been cases in which the courts have failed,
implicitly or explicitly,[1] to recognise the status of local
authorities or institutions of government. The period
1925-35 in particular has been characterised as one in
which the courts displayed a 'spirit of hostility to local
authority action'.[2]

From the mid 1930's, though, it is generally agreed that
this spirit of hostility was superceded by one of judicial
acquiescence to administrative decision-making and a
reluctance to intervene.[3] Indeed in the words of one
observer, the judges seemed on occasion:

> 'to be leaning over backwards almost to the point of
> falling off the Bench to avoid the appearance of
> hostility'.[4]

The classic judgment of this period was that of Lord
Greene MR in **Associated Provincial Picture Theatres Ltd. v.
Wednesbury Corporation**[5] in which he set out strict limits
on the powers of the courts to set aside an administrative

decision where the public authority concerned acted within its jurisdiction, emphasising that it was no part of the courts' function to replace the discretionary decision of the public authority with their own.

By the late 1970s, however, the distinction between those matters which fall within ministerial or local authority discretion and those within the competence of the courts to adjudicate became increasingly blurred.[6] Judicial self-limitation has given way to judicial activism and interventionism. For example, in **Secretary of State for Education and Science v Tameside Metropolitan B.C.**[7] the courts showed themselves prepared to overrule the decision of **one** public authority - the Minister, seeking to resist political change in favour of selective education - to the benefit in this instance of the discretion of the local council.

More recently it has been the decision-making processes of local authorities that were under scrutiny and challenge. There has been a growing inclination on the part of individuals and groups, including public bodies, to challenge local political decisions on legal grounds. This has been matched by the greater readiness on the part of courts to scrutinise much more closely the exercise of discretionary powers, particularly in the sphere of local government. This development is highlighted in the case of **Bromley L.B.C. v. Greater London Council**[8] (hereafter, the **GLC case**) which forms the starting point for this study and the book.

In the 1981 local elections the Labour Party was returned in London and the Metropolitan Counties committed to a manifesto of radical political change in order to respond to the problems of unemployment and social change in the decaying inner cities. When the new administration of the Greater London Council took office an early priority in their programme was to reduce public transport fares by 25 per cent. This reduction was to be accomplished by increasing the local authority's revenue support through an increase in "the rates". The legality of the decision of the new Council to implement its manifesto commitment by issuing a supplementary precept (of 6.1p in the pound to raise the necessary £69m) to local ratepayers was immediately tested by the Conservative-controlled Bromley London Borough Council in an application to the Divisional Court for judicial review. The object of this challenge, to the precept and the reduction in fares for which it was being raised was to prevent the increase in the costs of public transport being passed on to their ratepayers. Although the challenge was unsuccessful in the Divisional Court, it was upheld in the Court of Appeal and the House of Lords. This was partly on account of the interpretation given to the governing legislation and partly as a result of the way in which the decision was taken and its implications, not least that it left the ratepayers with the additional burden of meeting the consequentional loss of £50m in rate support grant.

The **GLC case** had an immediate impact on a number of other authorites responsible for public transport, requiring them hastily to reconsider their fares and subsidy policies. The parts of the judgments relating to grant penalties had an even wider effect, causing uncertainty throughout local government as to the legality of the general expenditure plans of local authorities.[9] Such concern followed from their awareness of a Conservative central government's commitment to acquire a detailed control over local expenditure as expressed in a succession of controversial grant reforms and Finance Acts which in turn has produced a consequential succession of legal challenges by individual authorities.[10] So to have some of its legislative reforms seeking to alter the emphasis and composition of local expenditure - for example, in relation to council house sales, housing subsidies and school transport.[11]

Local authorities, for their part, have similarly been examining the nature and limits of their legal powers as they have sought variously to increase the range or alter the form of services they provide. Such exercises of discretion and innovation have produced further legal actions - instigated in some instances by the council's own ratepayers or clients, and in some by other local authorities. Indeed, the **GLC case** is only one of a series of recent cases dealing with various aspects of local government. In a major review of contemporary legal developments in this field, Loughlin[12] has examined a number of cases concerned with local government finance and auditing, council house sales and rents, and education, and there has also been considerable court involvement in the last few years in issues of housing allocation and child care as well as in such traditionally 'judicialised' areas as planning.

These cases, like that of the **GLC**, illustrate a growing trend for local political decisions to be challenged on legal grounds. Disputes about the goals, content and merit of policies have come with increasing frequency to turn into controversies about the legality of the policy and the way in which it was adopted. The courts and the legal process have become, seemingly, a necessary part of political debate and decision-making. We term this the trend to 'judicialisation'.

Judicialisation defines the process of the courts and lawyers increasingly being drawn into administrative and politicial decision-making: the routines of taking counsel advice, issues having to be taken to court for a decision; and a substantive trend of the increasing use and application of legal concepts - such as "fiduciary duty", "standing" etc - in the discourse of decision-making. More generally judicialisation means administrative processes

3

becoming more court-like, more akin to a court process, whereby a case for action is based upon the preparation of meticulous reports of the relevant factors. This increasing involvement of local authorities with courts and lawyers is a natural consequence of the growth in **'juridification'**[13] which refers to an increasing concern with the legality of a local authority's decisions. Juridification defines the increasing inclination to examine, test, or give more precise definition to, the legal limits of, in our case, the powers of local authorities - on the part variously of central government, local authorities themselves, ratepayers, interest groups, and clients.

The research

Beyond noting the general concern caused by these developments within local government, little is known about the impact these judicial decisions have had on the internal workings and decision making of local authorities. Yet, as Loughlin has pointed out:

'Given the importance of long-established practice as a source of legitimacy in the British constitution, speculation on the impact of contemporary changes seem a particularly hazardous enterprise. Furthermore, before a task could be undertaken painstaking research would be needed to examine how recent developments are **actually** affecting local authorities'.[14]

Such research should distinguish between the short-term effect of specific judgments on the particular authority and/or policy area concerned in the case, and the wider and possibly longer-term judicial decisions might have in altering the policies and procedures of local government more generally and in heightening the sensitivites of local authority political leaders and officials to the possibility of legal challenge to their decisions through the courts.

Our proposal to the ESRC was to undertake preliminary research into the impact of judicial decisions in one specific policy field: public transport. We decided to focus immediately on public transport both because of its topicality following the **GLC** and related cases, and since, if research was not initiated at an early date, the opportunity for detailed empirical study of the effect of recent judicial decisions in this field would be missed, as some of the key metropolitan authorities were due to be abolished in 1985-6. While the study was directed at examining the impact of specific judgments within particular authorities, we also sought to explore the wider and possibly longer-term impact judicial activism may be having on local government, whether in terms of altering general decision-making processes and procedures of local authorities or in heightening the sensitivities of

4

political leaders and officials to the potential of legal challenge.

We proposed to base the preliminary research on a sample of metropolitan and non-metropolitan county authorities. Given the centrality of its policies in the context of recent legal developments in the field of public transport we regarded it as essential to include the GLC within our sample. In addition, we selected three of the six Metropolitan County Councils outside London, including authorities which faced specific legal challenges to their public transport policies in the wake of the **GLC case**. We also choose to include two non-Metropolitan County Councils in our sample as these authorities also have public transport responsibilities, the exercise of which may have been indirectly influenced by the **GLC** and related cases. These counties were chosen on the basis of their levels of expenditure on public transport taken in the light of their overall spending particularly as regards 'targets' set by central government: we also decided that one county should be a predominantly rural authority.

The research consisted of studies of documentary evidence relating to legal decisions on public transport, together with a series of interviews with senior local authority political leaders as well as officials. The interviews explored the history of each authority's public transport policy; the impact of the May 1981 local elections; the impact of the **GLC** and related cases on transport policy as well as upon other policy areas; and the general effect of judicialisation upon the organisation of local authorities and their decision-making processes. The interview schedules used in the research are reproduced in the Appendix.

Part I sets out the historical, political/administrative and legal/theoretical issues which provide a background to the study. In Part II we describe the court cases concerning transport in London and in the Metropolitan Counties and the extent to which there has been an impact of judicialisation upon the transport policies in the two non-Metropolitan Counties studied. We proceed analytically in Parts III and IV to discuss the implications of the court cases for legal processes and for the decision-making processes in local government.

Notes

1. E.g., **Roberts v. Hopwood** [1925] A.C. 578 and **Prescott v Birmingham Corporation** [1955] Ch. 210.

2. M. Loughlin, 'Administrative law, local government and the courts' in M. Loughlin **et al** (eds), **Half a Century of Municipal Decline 1935-85,** Allen & Unwin, 1985, p. 127.

3. **Ibid.,** p. 127.

4. J. A. G. Griffith, 'The law of property (land)' in M. Ginsberg (ed.), **Law and Opinion in England in the Twentieth Century,** Stevens, 1959, p. 120 - quoted in Loughlin **et al** (eds), **op. cit.,** p. 127.

5. [1948] 1 K.B. 223.

6. J. A. G. Griffith, **The Politics of the Judiciary,** 3rd ed., Fontana, 1986, pp. 131-32.

7. [1977] A.C. 1014.

8. [1982] 1 All E.R. 129. Only the judgments of the Court of Appeal and the House of Lords have been fully reported. The ruling of the Divisional Court is reported in **The Times,** November 11, 1981.

9. S. Marks, 'Law and Local Authorities', **Public Money,** June 1986.

10. E.g., **R. v. Secretary of State for the Environment, ex p. Brent L.B.C.** [1982] Q.B. 593; **R. v. Secretary of State for the Environment, ex p. Hackney L.B.C.** [1983] 1 W.L.R. 524 and [1984] 1 W.L.R. 592; **R. v. Secretary of State for the Environment, ex p. Leicester City Council** (1985) 25 R.V.R. 31; **R. v. Secretary of State for the Environment, ex p. GLC and ILEA** (1985, unreported); **Nottinghamshire** C.C. **v. Secretary of State for the Environment** [1986] 1 All E.R. 199.

11. See M. Loughlin, **Local Government in the Modern State,** Sweet and Maxwell, 1986, chs. 2-5.

12. M. Loughlin, **Local Government, The Law and the Constitution,** Local Government Legal Society Trust, 1983.

13. Loughlin, **op. cit.,** n. 11, chs. 1 and 9.

14. Loughlin, **op. cit.,** n. 12, p. 1.

PART I
THE CONTEXT OF
JUDICIAL CONTROL

2 The context of judicial control

1. The historical, political/administrative and socio-legal context of judicial control over local government

Although the main empirical focus of the study was on the impact of recent judicial decisions on the internal relations and decision-making of local authorities, we recognised the need to place this empirical work within a broader framework. In particular, we regarded it as vital that the study should from the outset begin to develop on an inter-disciplinary basis a general theory of the sources and incidence of legal challenges to local authorities and of the role of judicial review in the overall political, legal and administrative environment in which local authorities operate. Clearly, there would be a number of elements in any such general theory:

(a) Historical development of judicial control over local government

Periods of judicial activism/passivity and of constraint/flexibility toward local government can be related to other changes in the electoral, political and financial bases and conditions of local government.

  Obviously, one important factor to be considered in this connection is shifts in the political control of, or the incidence of party political organisation and divisions within, local authorities as an influence on the nature and incidence of legal challenges to local government. In his recent survey, Loughlin has observed that the period between 1910 and 1930:

'when local authorities in various parts of the country came under the control for the first time of Labour councillors, who sought to use local authority powers in novel ways'

was one of frequent judicial intervention at the behest of the Attorney General in the affairs of local government, and certainly this period was marked by a series of controversial cases involving the wider application of such concepts as 'fiducary duty' to constrain the activities of local authorities.[1] But, as Loughlin himself implies, it may be too narrow a view to relate such periods of judicial activism solely to party political conflicts between those in power centrally and within local government, and they might equally be traced to political differences between different local authorities or within particular authorities, to the development of strong public service unions within local government, to changes in the nature and scope of local authority duties and responsibilities, or in the perceived need for financial restraint on local government or in the economy as a whole.

Similarly, the sources of legal challenge to local authorities could be expected to have shifted over time, for example, in relation to the changing electoral base of local government or its wider service functions taking in different sections of the population and new interest groups. Thus, it might be hypothesised that while ratepayers and ratepayers' groups and other interested public authorities have been a traditional source of legal challenge in this field, it has only been in more recent times that other groups, such as parents affected by child care decisions, local authority tenants or homeless persons have begun to employ the law in this way. Developments in legal services and in 'public interest' conceptions of the law, as evidenced by the establishment of law centres, are clearly relevant to the emergence of these new sources of legal challenge.[2] At the same time, the recent cases involving legal challenge to local authorities may be seen as a sign of a revival of interest among more conservative political groups in the use of the law as a specific tool in a broader campaign of restricting the nature and scope of local authority services, and of government activity in general.[3]

While recognising the difficulties of tracing the specific sources of and influences on judicial decisions, it is important to explore whether judicial conceptions of and attitudes toward local government have altered in relation to these broader changes. Thus Loughlin has suggested that given the much wider scope of local authority services today as compared with earlier periods, and also changes in the tax and financial bases of local government, the concept of 'fiduciary duty' insofar as it implies a clear delineation and conflict of interests between ratepayers, on the one hand, and the recipients of local authority services on the other, may be outmoded and arbitrary in its application in particular cases.[4] This raises the question of whether there is evidence in past or recent cases of attempts by the judiciary to adapt the concept of 'fiduciary duty' or to develop alternatives to it (e.g., 'reasonableness' as a general criterion of Administrative Law) to better relate to the modern conditions of local government. On the other hand, the application of more traditional conceptions of 'fiduciary duty' in recent cases may itself reflect a concern or bias on the part of some elements of the judiciary to re-impose a more limited definition of the proper nature and scope of local government activities.

(b) The changing economic, political and institutional
    context of local government

It can be argued that it was the failure of the judiciary in the **GLC case** to have sufficient understanding of or regard for the implications of their judgments in the context of the new rate support grant system that was one of the main causes of the resultant uncertainty created in local government.[5] The **GLC case** and its aftermath thus clearly illustrated the need to relate the effects stemming from judicial interventions to those arising from other sources of control over local government, such as central administrative and financial regulation or that imposed under the recently reformed local government audit system,[6] as well as to the constraints on local authorities stemming from wider changes in the economy and society. For example, the recent developments impinging on local government include, in terms of **economic change**, the ending of growth and resultant effects in restricting public spending and local authority expenditure in particular, and at the same time structural changes in the nature of work and employment markets driven by the new technologies, leading to new demands on local government in its economic development role[7] and other service sectors. In terms of **political change** there has been a fragmentation of political interests within and between parties and interest groups, possibly reflecting differential interpretations of appropriate responses to the problems of structural change in the economy and its social effects. Clearly, these wider developments have had major implications in terms of **institutional change**, most importantly in the relations between central and local government and the increased use of financial, administrative, political and legal devices to control local authorities and undermine their autonomy.[8]

Within this overall context of particular interest is the relationship and shifting emphasis between **legal accountability** of local authorities and of councillors and officials for their actions, as exercised ultimately through the courts: **administrative/financial control** imposed on them from central government and possibly other 'independent' agencies (e.g., the Commissions for Local Government Administration and the Local Government Audit Commission); and their **political accountability** to their

11

electorates through the institutions of local democracy. Although the distinction between these different forms of accountability may not be so clear-cut in practice, nevertheless both legal theorists[9] and political scientists[10] have portrayed them as potentially in conflict with one another. Thus, central government administrative and financial control, to the extent that it operates outside the scope of predetermined rules and formal procedures, has been seen as in tension with strict legal accountability. Ironically, however, it may be that one effect of recent judicial decisions re-asserting traditional notions of legal accountability of local authorities has been, either through direct changes brought about in local authority policies and/or procedures or indirectly in the uncertainty resulting from these cases, to reinforce the effectiveness of central government administrative and financial controls over local government. For example, there is evidence to suggest that in the wake of the **GLC case** many local authorities readily accepted advice from the Department of the Environment regarding the legality of their spending plans, despite its dubious basis in legal opinion.[11] To the extent that this reinforcement of central control has occurred, it is of course arguable that a further effect of recent judicial decisions has been to undermine the effectiveness of local authorities' political accountability at a time when new political demands are arising from their electorates as a result of broader economic developments.

That these results might have emerged from the system of legal challenge to local authorities raises the issue of how far the structures through which legal accountability operates themselves incorporate an ideological and/or organisational bias in favour of certain interests. There is a close parallel to be drawn in this respect between current developments in respect of local government generally and earlier work by McAuslan on the ideological interests built into the system of land use planning decision-making[12] or that of Bridges, following McAuslan, on the interests implicit in different forms of public inquiry.[13] Thus, McAuslan has suggested that whatever the tensions and attendant compromises required between private property interests with their commitment to strict legal control over planning and governmental decisions and planners and administrators with their interest in the flexibility of governmental action in the name of a wider public good, there is nevertheless a 'common interest' between them:

'in combating the ideology and practice of public participation, for just as the ideology threatens the power and position of the bureaucracy in government so it also threatens the power and position of private property in society'.[14]

12

More generally, in his seminal article Galanter[15] has argued that, leaving such specific ideological biases aside, the very structure and organisation of the legal system in terms of access to the courts and the operation of their procedures, has the effect of favouring certain mainly organised interests. Galanter's analysis has obvious applicability in attempting to assess the relative advantages and disadvantages facing different groups, say between ratepayers' interests as represented by local industrialists and those of the recipients of local authority services as represented by a tenants' association or individual, in their use of the law as a means of exerting pressure on local authorities.[16] Similar consideration will also be relevant in attempting to assess the impact of judicial decisions within local authorities.

(c) Developments in Administrative/Public Law

As is implied in much of the above discussion, it is essential to take account not only of changes in local government but also in the field of Administrative Law generally, including recent attempts by several writers to formulate more radical or critical theories of Public Law. Viewed from this perspective, judicial activism in relation to local government is part of a broader development of administrative law in England over the past twenty-five years or so. This period has seen judicial review of administrative action, in particular, develop both in practice and as a discrete subject area within the academic study of law, as marked by specialist courses and text books. Underlying this development have been attempts to formulate or distil from cases a set of general principles applicable to the administrative process. Some acceptance of this approach by the legal profession can be seen in the inclusion for the first time in **Halsbury's Laws of England** of a heading 'Administrative Law' in 1973[17] and perhaps more significant in the determination of the Judicial Committee of the House or Lords that almost all challenges to the legality of administrative actions should be heard on 'an application for judicial review'[18] in the Divisional Court of the Queen's Bench Division, such cases being assigned to the recently created Crown Office List so that they will be heard by judges having an Administrative Law background.

Although such developments cannot be controverted, there is still scope for doubt as to both the general applicability of the 'principles' distilled by the case-law process and subsequent academic writing and also their observance in practice. Our research on the impact of judicial decisions on local authorities can be relevant to this debate. Thus, if it were found that the effect of particular decisions tended to be confined to the specific authorities or policy areas involved, this in itself would raise questions as to the existence of a general Administrative Law as opposed to more limited public laws in different policy sectors. Nor would the implications of the research be purely theoretical. By examining the extent to which decisions about the 'fiduciary duty' to ratepayers in formulating transport policy,[19] (or decisions about the right to a hearing before taxi licenses are granted,[20] or remarks about the need for adequate evidence for the exercise of education powers[21]) influence the operation of the administrative process in other subject areas and other local authorities, some light can be shed on the practicality of formulating general principles. In so doing the study can play a part in evaluating the feasibility of a Code of Administrative Procedure of the type found at state and federal levels in the United States, a proposal for the introduction of which in this country has been considered on a number of occasions.[22]

We are aware that there has developed over the past few years, to some extent in opposition to the type of administrative law thinking outlined above, an attempt by various writers to formulate more radical or critical public law theories. Perhaps most notable among these writers has been McAuslan[23] and, more recently, Prosser.[24] These writers have sought to look outside the narrow confines of case law and other strictly legal sources, turning instead to broader political and social theories[25] and to radical forms of social and political activities around public policy issues in order to derive more critical principles against which to evaluate the actions of public bodies. Indeed, a common feature of these theorists is the view that principles of Administrative Law derived from case law and procedures and practices that may be based upon them cannot be assumed to have universal acceptability, precisely because they are likely to incorporate ideological biases, such as that in favour of private property, built into the legal system generally. Unfortunately, there is little evidence as yet of this type of theorisation moving beyond its critical stance in order to make positive recommendations as to the types of procedures and practices that might better fulfil the broader ideals of participation and accountability that have been identified as key organising principles, and Prosser himself acknowledges that there is a need for further theoretical development, especially around the concept of power:

> 'for this provides key background to the organising concepts by pointing to where participation and accountability are necessary to mediate the effects of the exercise of power, and to the forces which may defeat their application in practice'.[26]

All of the writers within this radical or critical Public Law school have recognised the need for empirical research, and we see our investigation as directly relevant to this demand. In particular, the research has enabled us to examine within the field of local government the broader

14

political effects stemming from the imposition through judicial decisions of Administrative Law principles and of procedures based upon them.

2.   Developing an analytical framework

So far our discussions have focussed on the general contextual issues outlined in Section I above, and we are aware of the need, before proceeding to discuss our detailed empirical work on the impact of judicial decisions on local authorities to develop an analytical framework in which to place this work and to develop more specific research hypotheses. This analytical framework is designed to conceptualise the relative influences on decision-making within local authorities when set against the wider economic, political and institutional constraints operating on local government as a whole. Thus, we envisage this analytical framework as incorporating elements of both an 'action' perspective with its emphasis on actors striving for power in order to facilitate their interests, and a 'structuralist' perspective with its stress on institutional and environmental constraints which limit the operations of power. We contend that to base explanation entirely within either of these two perspectives, in terms of unfettered agency on the one hand or abstract structures on the other, would lead to an unwarranted simplification[27] of the complexity of decision-making in local government.

Our analysis begins with the assumption that the interpretive procedures of actors within local authorities would be central to understanding their response to recent judicial decisions. Amongst the different officers and councillors we expect to find varying perceptions and understandings of the law in general and of doctrines such as **ultra vires**, these variations being related to the policy area in which the particular actor was concerned. For example, it is likely that the perceptions of law will differ as between, say, planning with a fairly established tradition of legal challenge to local authority decisions, and education or social services where until recently there was less experience and expectation of judicial intervention. Evidence of these different perceptions might be found in the frequency of resort to legal advice in decision making; in the sources of such advice, whether internal to the authority or from auditors or outside counsel (in which case the selection of counsel will also be relevant) and in the interpretations of and significance attached to such legal opinions once received. Of course, this type of analysis of internal actors' perceptions of the law needs to be sensitively related to changing interpretations within the legal community generally of the importance, for example, of the concept of 'fiduciary duty'.

Formal or informal advice on such matters received from other external sources, in particular central government, can also be considered. More broadly, we expect that underlying and shaping actors' perceptions and interpretations of the law and of the legal effect of judicial decisions would be a set of beliefs, values and ideologies which they hold about the law itself, about the management of local authorities and about the purposes, status and accountability of public services. Those lawyers who see individual cases as contributing to a general body of principles will act differently from those who consider the view that judicial decisions relate only to specific cases; those officers and councillors who value the corporate responsibility of their local authorities for the overall cultural, economic and social well-being of their communities may respond to judicial decisions in a different way from those committed to the provision of separate services within statutory limits; those actors ideologically committed to public services will seek different interpretations of the law from those whose belief systems commend manageralism and administrative efficiency. As indicated previously, the work of McAuslan[28] in particular on the role of ideology and attitudes regarding property, public service and participation in influencing interpretations and the operation of planning law is instructive in this regard. Also, ideological differences need to be related to party and factional divisions among councillors and to variations in professional backgrounds among officers, as well as to their past experiences and positions held within the hierarchy of local authority organisation and decision-making.

This latter factor points to the analytical importance of the concept of power, as stressed both by political scientists[29] and critical Public Law theorists such as Prosser.[30] Not only will the extent to which different values and beliefs influence decision-making vary according to the actors' relative positions of power and domination within local authorities, but the effect of increased judicial activity may be to alter power relations within local authorities, but the effect of increased judicial activity may be to alter power relations within local authorities in favour of certain actors. Thus, beyond any specific policy changes that may result from particular judicial decisions, they may lead to the introduction of new procedures which, following on from Galanter[31], will themselves bring certain values and considerations to the fore and possibly strengthen the position within the decision-making process of those actors with access to counsel or other sources of legal advice such as auditors, with knowledge about the courts and law, and with skill to interpret legal judgements. It is also important to explore the 'hidden' aspects of power: not only the ability to 'make decisions' but also the capacity to define the key issues, to shape agenda and to institutionalise legal understandings and values as 'the way things are done here'.[32]

Yet, the operation of power and the potential discretion of actors will themselves be constrained by existing institutional arrangements and environmental conditions impinging on particular authorities and on local government as a whole. Renewed emphasis is likely to be given to the position of local authorities as creatures of statute only having powers conferred on them by statute. In this connection it may be noted that as recently as 1981 Elliott argued for a reconceptualisation of the legal base of local government around the notion of **dominium** as opposed to **imperium** powers,[33] and this probably reflected a tendency within local government, derived from earlier structural and management changes to obscure the legal boundaries of local authority powers and to make considerations of the legality (vires) a more peripheral factor in the overall decision making process. However, Loughlin has contended that the implication of recent case law, particularly as regards rate support grant, has been to re-assert the **imperium** bases of local government powers,[34] and this may have led authorities to tie their decisions more closely to the limits of the statutory framework. But as previously emphasised, account needs to be taken of the other pressures and constraints on local authorities, particularly in terms of the balance of local party politics and economic, political and administrative relations with central government.

Notes

1. M. Loughlin, **Local Government, The Law and the Constitution**, Local Government Society Trust, 1983, p. 91.

2. See M. Partington 'Public Interest Law', 1979, **LAG Bulletin**, pp. 225-7.

3. J. D. Stewart, **Local Government: The Conditions of Local Choice**, Allen and Unwin, 1983.

4. Loughlin, **op.cit.**, p 93.

5. For a detailed discussion of this point, see **ibid.**, ch. 3.

6. **Ibid.**, chap 6 and O Lomas, 'Audit Law and Audit Law Reform - Some Implications for Local Government', 9 **Journal of Local Government Policy Making** 45 (1982).

7. See, for example, M. Grant 'Law, Policy and Fallacy in Central/Local Relations', Paper given at SPTL Administrative Law Group's Annual Meeting, University of Birmingham, 3 April 1982.

8. Stewart, **op.cit.**

9. For recent discussions of the issue of accountability by lawyers see T. Prosser, 'Towards a Critical Public Law' 9, **Journal of Law and Society** 1 (1981) and Loughlin, **op.cit.**, ch. 7.

10. **cf.** the discussion of concepts of control and accountability in relation to quangos in N. Johnson, 'Quangos and the Structure of British Government', **Public Administration**, Winter, 1979, pp. 379-95.

11. Loughlin, **op.cit.**, ch. 2.

12. P. McAuslan, **The Ideologies of Planning Law**, Pergamon, 1980.

13. L. T. Bridges, 'Political, Administrative and Judicial Functions of Planning Inquiries' in **Aspects of Anglo-Canadian and Quebec Administrative Law**, Laval University, Quebec, 1979.

14. McAuslan, **op.cit.**, p. 265.

15. M. Galanter, 'Why the 'Hares' Come Out Ahead: Speculations on the Limits of Legal Change' 9 **Law and Society Review** 95 (1974).

16. For one of the few studies of collective legal action among such groups, see A. Stewart, **Housing Action in an Industrial Suburb**, Academic Press, 1981.

17. 4th ed., Butterworths, 1973, vol. 1.

18. **O'Reilly v. Mackman** [1982] 3 All. E.R. 1124.

19. **Bromley L.B.C. v. GLC** [1982] 1 All E.R. 129, **R. v. Merseyside County Council, ex p. Great Universal Stores,** (1982) 80 L.G.R. 639; **R. v. London Transport Executive, ex p. GLC,** [1983] 2 All. E.R. 262.

20. **R. v. Liverpool Corporation, ex p. Liverpool Taxi Fleet Operators' Association** [1975] 2 Q.B. 299.

21. **Secretary of State for Education v. Tameside M.B.C.** [1977] A.C. 1014.

22. **Discussion Paper** (April 1981), p. 68.

23. McAuslan, **op.cit.**

24. Prosser, **op.cit.**

25. McAuslan has drawn much of his thinking on this subject from C. B. Macpherson, **The Life and Times of Liberal Democracy,** Oxford University Press, 1977, while Prosser has relied on Jurgen Habermas' **Towards a Rational Society,** Heinemann Eduational, 1971, and **Legitimation Crisis,** Heinemann Educational, 1976.

26. Prosser, **op.cit.,** p. 12.

27. S. Ranson, B. Hinings and R. Greenwood, 'The Structuring of Organisation Structures', **Administrative Science Quarterly,** March 1980. P. Dunleavy, **Urban Politics Analysis,** Macmillan, 1980.

28. McAuslan, **op.cit.**

29. S. Lukes, **Power: A Radical View,** Macmillan, 1974. P. Saunders, **Urban Politics,** Hutchinson, 1979, Dunleavy, **op.cit.**

30. Prosser, **op.cit.**

31. Galanter, **op.cit.**

32. Saunders, **op.cit.**

33. M. Elliott, **The Role of Law in Central-Local Relations,** ERSC, 1981.

34. Loughlin, **op.cit.**, p 81. For further discussion see O. Lomas 'Law as a resource and the resourcefulness of law' in S. Ranson, G. W. Jones and K. Walsh (eds) **Between Centre and Locality: The Politics of Public Policy,** Allen and Unwin, 1985.

PART II
THE NARRATIVE
ACCOUNT

3 Transport in London

Between 1969 and 1984 the Transport (London) Act 1969 placed the GLC under a duty to develop policies that would promote the provision of 'integrated, efficient and economic' transport facilities and services in Greater London. That Act gave the responsibility for the actual operation of the transport facilities and services to the London Transport Executive (LTE). Up to 1981 the GLC had used its power under section 3(1) of the 1969 Act to make grants to the Executive as a way of providing a modest amount of revenue support or subsidy. The actual level of grant varied but tended to be greater when the GLC was controlled by Labour. Although it had been cut back by the 1978-81 Conservative-controlled Council, this was because revenue support was seen as a slippery slope that promoted inefficiency and sustained unnecessary transport services and not on account of any concern for the legality of such support. In common with its election campaign in other metropolitan areas in 1981, the Labour Party in London had a manifesto commitment to secure a reduction in public transport fares through an increase in revenue support. There was an undertaking to reduce them by 25 per cent.

However, the newly-elected Labour Council's pursuit of their manifesto policies of expanding public services to meet local needs and demands brought them into direct conflict with the Conservative Government and its commitment to contracting public expenditure. For local authorities this not only meant reductions in the level of Rate Support Grant (RSG) they could expect to receive from central government but also, as a result of the Local Government Act 1980, new controls upon the level of local expenditure. Under the new system of (block grant) assessments and targets for spending local authorities could expect to lose grant in proportion to the degree that they exceeded spending targets. The expenditure implications of manifesto policies could, therefore, significantly affect the financial demands upon ratepayers if the policy took the authority's budget over the target level thus reducing the level of expected RSG support and thus increasing the 'price' of the policy to the ratepayer. The point is well made by Maurice Stonefrost, the GLC's then Comptroller of Finance in a talk to the Oxford Faculty of Law:

> "In administrative terms, there was not an open direct conflict between the general financial presumptions underlying the Labour Party's manifesto and the Government's policy. However the government was using a powerful indirect financial instrument to further its expenditure policy. The higher the net revenue expenditure of the GLC became, the lower the amount of general block grant. The relative effect, in cash terms upon the ratepayers of marginal increases in expenditure can properly be described as dramatic ... London ratepayers had to pay two prices for a decision to increase expenditure. The price of the decision itself and a 'penalty price' to Government for taking the decision by way of reduction in grant. The cost to ratepayers of the application of the newly elected Council carrying out a policy not supported by Government was ... (a) 'penalty price' nearly double the actual decision price. It is therefore clear that any variation from Government targets raises the issue of reasonableness (of the local authority's expenditure policies)".[1]

In London the reduction in fares would have to be achieved through a supplementary precept of 6.1p in the pound to raise the necessary £69m.

It was against this background that the GLC faced a direct challenge from Bromley London Borough Council to the legality of the precept and the reduction in fares. Proceedings were commenced in September 1981 and within three months the case had been heard by the Divisional Court, the Court of Appeal and the House of Lords. Although the action of the GLC was upheld in the Divisional Court, the precept and the reduction in fares were condemned as unlawful by both appeal courts. This outcome was a considerable surprise for both the Labour members and the senior officers of the GLC since neither had had any serious doubts about the legality of the action taken. When the policy of reducing fares had been adopted the Labour Party in London was aware that a supplementary precept would be required. This did not, however, give rise to any concern about its legality since the members were mindful of the debates in Parliament preceding the enactment of the 1969 Act. Their understanding was that the GLC was intended to run London Transport and they relied on the fact that the Act said it could give grants for any purpose. As one member put it:

'If the grant by the GLC was a burden on the ratepayers then that was to be a matter for them'.

The making of a grant was thus seen as an electoral and not a legal issue. Nor did the question of legality really arise during the election campaign, although one officer did recall it being voiced, without any impact, by a former Conservative transport committee chairman.

After the election the new council had sought to implement the public transport policy speedily and indeed fares were reduced by 25 per cent within five months. In a matter of days after the election London Transport had been asked to produce a range of options on ways of achieving a 25 per cent reduction in fares and then there was public consultation through meetings in each of the eight bus districts. The final choice was made on 21st July, to be implemented in October, and the supplementary precept was issued the following day. At this time it became clear that proposals by the government to curb local authority spending might lead to a loss of rate support grant if the GLC increased its expenditure on public transport. The GLC was warned by one officer that this would make the reduction in fares more expensive but it resolved to implement its proposal in spite of the possibility of this extra financial burden. This gave that officer pause for thought:

'When you get to the point where in order to do something you are going to end up paying four times as much because of the grant penalties, then you have to think about it. I felt that the thing you were doing had to be of such importance that you couldn't postpone it, or you had to be in a position where you could see a way of reducing the costs in a short period, to justify it. Neither of these conditions applied.

This left the question of whether I should take it on myself to express an opinion on a possible breach of fiduciary duty or whether, if challenged, we would be held in breach of a fiduciary duty. I knew if I wrote what I have just said it would be decisive or would invite a legal challenge, so I didn't. I thought that there were two unreasonablenesses - the first by central government in imposing penalties, and the second by the local authority in the exercise of its discretion. I felt that the responsibility rested with the elected authority and their intentions had been well and truly signalled in the election. I felt that that was superior to any doubts I might have, so I kept quiet'.

These were, of course, only doubts as to the legality of the grant in the particular circumstances of government spending curbs and not as to the principle of a grant of this magnitude. In the event the question of legality did not feature in the advice sought and obtained from the officers on the implementation of the transport policy. Indeed the legal department was not even involved but it did not perceive any legal problems to exist. It shared the view of other officers and the members that the grant and the necessary precept were within the GLC's statutory powers. This view was, of course, confirmed by the decision of the Divisional Court in the **GLC case** and as one member put it in response to his own question about why there was no legal advice sought before the manifesto was adopted or implementation began:

'What better legal advice was there than the High Court?'.

In other words any advice sought would have been the same as the ruling in the Divisional Court. That court's ready confirmation of the view prevailing amongst members and officers makes it easy to understand why, without being complacent, the Bromley challenge was not taken too seriously at the outset.

They were undoubtedly fortified in their confidence that the outcome of the proceedings would be favourable by the unwillingness of other Conservative-controlled councils to 'waste' money in joining the challenge by Bromley and by the fact, according to one officer, that the Bromley officers also expected the case to be unsuccessful. Bromley's initial allegations were that there had been a failure to take account of relevant factors (particularly the possibility of being 'penalised' by loss of rate support grant) and consideration of irrelevant ones (notably the manifesto commitment). The GLC's legal department was not impressed with the way in which Bromley's application for judicial review was framed and, although the allegations were developed in the course of the proceedings, it expected to be able to defend the action successfully and in particular to meet the implications that the GLC had approached the decision with a closed mind. At this stage the members were not very much involved or concerned with the case but they and the legal department were naturally happy when the Divisional Court upheld the validity of the grant and the precept on the ground that it was:

'Impossible on the whole of the evidence to say that no reasonable council could not have come to the same conclusion as the GLC'. (Dunn LJ)

However, the case went almost immediately to the Court of Appeal, where it was heard by Lord Denning MR and Lords Justices Oliver and Watkins, and for the first time the provisions of the 1969 Act came under really close scrutiny. This arose more through the intervention of Lord Justice Oliver than the argument of Bromley and this was something for which the council was not entirely prepared. As one officer commented:

> 'Oliver's interjections were not always clear as to their consequences - deliberately so. We would have needed more time to have picked up the point'.

In the Divisional Court the argument had been about the way in which the decision of the GLC had been reached and whether the particular grant was so arbitrary as to be invalid. The Court of Appeal's judgments, in ruling the precept and the grant to be **ultra vires,** rested on both the way in which the decision had been reached (particularly the speed and the commitment to the election manifesto) and on whether there was actually the power to subsidise the transport system in London through advance grants. Its construction of the Act was to rule that London Transport had to endeavour to run the system on an economic basis or in accordance with business principles and only if that failed could the GLC help it to balance its budget by a grant. Both members and officers were surprised to lose and especially on the second ground which one officer described as:

> 'An Alice in Wonderland construction of the 1969 Act'.

At this point members became much more involved in the legal strategy and there was some suggestion that there should be a publicity campaign attacking the Court of Appeal decision. However, they accepted advice from officers and counsel that a public campaign might not be appreciated by the House of Lords. There were thus no threats to break the law and pay the grant, something for which they were attacked for not doing by their supporters. Comment in the press at the time concentrated more on Lord Denning's judgment and its strong attack on the GLC's adherence to the election manifesto but the point about the interpretation of the 1969 Act was to prove to be more important in the House of Lords and in shaping the GLC's initial response to the holding that the grant and the precept were **ultra vires.**

Although the Court of Appeal decision was a major setback it was nonetheless expected that it would be reversed on appeal and this attitude was maintained throughout the hearing and up until judgment. The officers certainly remained convinced 'that the GLC would come out on top' and it was felt that they had been well represented and had 'won all the arguments'. The ruling in favour of Bromley by the House of Lords came, therefore, as a considerable shock to everyone. Four of their Lordships[2] held the grant and the precept to be invalid primarily because there was only power to make good unavoidable losses and not to

further a particular social policy. This, it was held, was
the consequence of London Transport's statutory duty to run
its operations on ordinary business principles. Only Lord
Diplock considered that there was power to make the grant
although he also held it invalid as a breach of the
GLC's fiduciary duty to its ratepayers because they were
forced to suffer an increased financial burden without any
corresponding increase in transport services.

Some of the officers could have accepted, while
disagreeing, losing on the second ground but to lose on the
issues of construction was clearly traumatic and almost
three years afterwards feelings were still bitter. The
defeat seemed much easier for the members to cope with as
the House of Lords' judgments were deemed political and
inspired the 'Can't Pay, Won't Pay' campaign[3] led by some
members when the rates were ultimately increased. The
members thus had very few illusions about the courts. For
the officers, on the other hand, defeat in the House of
Lords was incomprehensible. As one officer put it:

> 'It seems to me that it was self-evident, without
> knowing anything about public transport, what the
> structure of the Act meant in its own right. You could
> derive that from the placing of the parts, even if you
> weren't dealing with a piece of legislation but were
> writing Winnie-the-Pooh. It was self-evident that the
> Act was hierarchical ... The Act was so very much
> different from previous public transport Acts. You
> couldn't help to ask why it was so different. I can't
> understand how it was possible for the Law Lords to
> read the Act the way they did'.

For another officer:

> 'The decision of the House of Lords was impossible to
> arrive at rationally'.

For some officers the way in which courts work added
frustration to the sense of incomprehension:

> 'The things that disturbed one about the process was
> that the evidence of transport in other cities was
> ignored and that games were played around not having
> regard to Hansard'.[4]

As another officer put it:

> "an opaque screen stood between Parliament's discussion
> and a 'value-free Act'".

There was also unhappiness that, on the question of the
grant being a breach of the GLC's fiduciary duty to the
ratepayers, an important dimension was excluded from the
process:

'The change in central/local government relations has altered the parameters of unreasonableness. A new set of tests were needed, as central government has rendered it impossible to act reasonably. But to take this on would have been to put central government on trial and this the judge wouldn't do'.

Even the attitude of the courts to the way in which the GLC's decisions were reached was seen as unrealistic given the way in which local government was organised:

'The problem comes when the decision-making processes of local government are held up against the decision-making processes of judicial review and of the audit. Decision-making in local government is carried out by officers bringing before members matters requiring decision - it is the members, who are lay people, who have to take the decisions. They don't have the ability, officers or members, to spend five days on an issue and examine in the same detail as occurs in judicial review, arguing over the meaning of a word, different views on particular aspect, etc'.

There is no doubt that the experience left the officers disenchanted with the intervention of the courts. Although this is a phenomenon observed with respect to many losing defendants, in this instance it reflected a genuine surprise about the difference between the court's approach to the law and their own perception of it.

Nevertheless, after the decision of the House of Lords, the GLC was faced with the task of complying with it. One member said of the period immediately afterwards:

'There was a shell-shock response. They had no option but to cut services and raise fares - relying on a break-even basis, that is, fares to be increased until any further increase would lower the total income'.

The decision to raise fares was taken but very soon afterwards both members and officers found themselves under pressure to take a broader view of the GLC's power to give grants than they had thought was allowed under the House of Lords ruling. Some members did not believe that an increase in fares was the only way to react but neither officers nor other members were prepared to do anything else. This was a very frustrating period for those members who believed there must be some other way as, although the only advice they received from officers was that there was no alternative, a variety of pressure groups and borough councils were saying that there was a way to produce a transport plan with lower fares. The senior officers were taking what they thought was the only approach permissible under the 1969 Act as interpreted by the House of Lords but soon found that almost everyone else was saying that there was more latitude. As one officer told us:

29

'Within a week of the House of Lords' decision there were only three of us who interpreted the judgment in a harsh way ... We were presumed to be overcautious as bureaucrats. No party to the whole thing had an interest in interpreting the Law Lords the way we did. But our view was coloured by the knowledge that the Law Lords had made their decision in the light of the case we had presented. But all the other parties used the phrase 'as far as practical' to undermine our interpretation. The mood had changed - no one was after the destruction of the transport service in London'.

The divergence between the outside advice being given to members and the view taken by the officers was the source of tension between them. This, together with an indication by the London Borough of Camden that it would take the GLC to court if there was no reduction in fares gave rise to pressure by councillors for a change in counsel to someone who could provide a way out. The person chosen was Roger Henderson, QC who had successfully represented several London Boroughs in a challenge to alterations in the Rate Support Grant scheme. On his advice they entered into a long process to get the fares that they wanted, relying on their power to give the Executive directions as to the exercise and performance of their functions 'in relation to matters appearing to the Council to affect the policies and measures which it is the duty of the Council ... to develop, organise or carry out'.[5] He told them that:

'They had to form policies and then a plan, then to take account of the relevant considerations including the ratepayers and then using a balanced plan to give the London Transport Executive directions'.

This led to a fundamentally different approach in the method of working and considerable involvement by the legal department:

'We were involved on a daily basis during the build up to the Direction over several months. We worked closely throughout with Henderson so that reports leading to the Direction were properly prepared. This involved going through all the reports, the draft plan, making sure there were full consultations and consideration of options. Every facet of the work was carried out in consultation with and advice from counsel'.

A Direction requiring London Transport to restructure its fares which would lead to a loss in revenue that would be covered by an increase in the GLC grant was produced and London Transport were advised that it was unlawful. The GLC then sought a declaration that the Direction was lawful, although there was less confidence this time in the outcome. As one officer put it:

'I was confident of a good case, well-founded and well-researched and one that was welcomed by the London Transport Executive but I was uncertain about how the law would work'.

The Divisional Court, relying on a broader interpretation of the House of Lords' decision than the officers had themselves adopted, granted the declaration sought.[6] London Transport, who had wanted to comply with the direction if it could be shown to be lawful, did not appeal and the restructuring of fares then took place.

Although the restrictive analysis of the GLC's powers under the 1969 Act had been the main complaint about the House of Lords' decision in the **GLC case**, both it and the success in the action for a declaration demonstrated the importance of procedure and the need to have legal advice. This remains a feature of the GLC's working practice. As one officer put it:

'First, we generate a lot more paper. Second, there is more - longer writing down of relevant factors and irrelevant factors in decisions. We are now setting down many things that were previously implicitly understood. Third, we obtain counsel's opinion more often. Four, the leading politicians have easily learnt how to show that they have taken account of all relevant factors and not the irrelevant ones'.

The issue of legality is now at the front of everyone's mind and legal advice, whether from within or without the GLC, is readily sought in order to "play safe". This does not mean, however, that the GLC was unwilling to test the limits of its powers. On the contrary it felt able to break new ground as legal advice has resolved uncertainties about the limits of its discretion. These issues will be discussed further in Chapters 7 and 8. The GLC, however, lost its responsibility for public transport following the enactment of the London Regional Transport Act 1984 and has itself now been abolished.

Notes

1. 'An Administrator's Viewpoint on **R. v. GLC, ex p. Bromley L.B.C.**' (March 2, 1983), pp. 3-4.

2. Lords Wilberforce, Keith of Kinkel, Scarman and Brandon.

3. In which passengers were encouraged not to pay the higher fares introduced following the House of Lords' ruling in the **GLC case**.

4. Court, will not refer to parliamentary debates as an aid to the interpretation of statutes.

5. Transport (London) Act 1969, s. 11(1).

6. **R. v. London Transport Executive, ex p. GLC** [1983] 2 All E.R. 262.

4 Transport in the Metropolitan Counties

In this chapter we turn to public transport policy outside London and we consider specifically the impact of the House of Lords' decision in the **GLC case** on the fares policies of the six Metropolitan County Councils. The nature of that impact, as we shall see, turned at least in part on the fact that, both before and since local government reorganisation in the early 1970s, transport policy in these major conurbations was governed by different legislation from that in Greater London. To a greater extent than even the progenitors of the legislation may have appreciated at the time, the Transport (London) Act 1969 differed in certain key respects from the Transport Act 1968 which preceded it.

That 1968 Act established Passenger Transport Areas covering four conurbations outside London - West Midlands, Greater Manchester, Merseyside and Tyneside. This was, of course, prior to (though, it was argued, without prejudice to) the report of the Redcliffe-Maud Royal Commission [1]. In these four conurbations Passenger Transport Authorities (PTAs), consisting of representatives of the constituent local authorities, were formed with responsibility for developing public transport policy in their areas. These policies were to be carried out by Passenger Transport Executives (PTEs),which employed a professional and manual workforce and were responsible for the management of the service. With local government reorganisation in 1974, the six metropolitan county councils (and in Scotland the Strathclyde Regional Council) became PTAs, and two new PTEs were therefore established - in South and West Yorkshire.

Under the key section 9(3) of the Transport Act 1968, these PTAs and PTEs were charged with a duty:

'to secure or promote the provision of a properly **integrated** and **efficient system** of public passenger transport to meet the needs of that area **with due regard** to the town planning and traffic and parking policies of the councils of constituent areas and to **economy** and safety of **operation'**. (our emphases)

It will be seen that there is a subtle, but potentially crucial, distinction between the wording of this section and that of section 1 of the Transport (London) Act 1969, under which it was the GLC's duty to 'promote the provision of **integrated, efficient and economic transport** facilities and services for Greater London' (our emphases). Whether intentionally or not, the term 'economy' in the 1968 Act could be interpreted as being a somewhat more subordinate and qualified consideration than in the 1969 Act's wording.

There were other minor differences as well [2], but it must be emphasised that prior to the **GLC case** few, if any, members or officers in the Metropolitan Counties had given any thought whatever to such semantics. Nor are they an overriding concern of our research which was principally with the longer term and more general impact of judicial decisions on the decision-making processes and practices of local authorities. Before these longer-term developments can be examined, though, it is both important and necessary to look at the immediate impact of a judgment as fundamental and potentially far-reaching as that of the House of Lords in the **GLC case.**

The term 'immediate' and the time-scale associated with it can, at least, in this instance, be quite precisely specified. Bromley's challenge to the GLC's cheap fares policy went first to the Divisional Court at the end of October 1981. The unanimous Court of Appeal ruling, overturning that of the Divisional Court, came on 10th November 1981, and the House of Lords' judgment some five weeks later on 17th December 1981. The only case involving any of the Metropolitan Counties actually to be argued through the courts was the challenge by Great Universal Stores Ltd. (GUS) to Merseyside County Council's fares policy and the supplementary rate precept associated with it. Mr Justice Woolf's judgment in this case, **R. v. Merseyside County Council, ex p. Great Universal Stores Ltd.,** which dismissed GUS's application for judicial review seeking an order of certiorari to quash the Council's supplementary precept, was delivered on 17th February 1982. [3]. The time period under consideration in this chapter, therefore, is one of almost exactly two months, between the middle of December 1981 and the middle of February 1982.

34

The main outline of events can be quite easily recounted using information that was either publicly available at the time or which has since become available. [4]. What cannot be conveyed from such an outline, though, is any real sense of the pressures and uncertainties which surrounded the decisions taken, the incomplete information and the frequently conflicting advice that was available to those involved in the decision-making processes, and, of course, the attitudes and perceptions of some of the key participants themselves. It was this depth and breadth of perspective that we were able to fill out through out interviews with some of those participants in three of the six Metropolitan Counties, and with the assistance of some of the additional documentary material they were prepared to make available to us. Extracts from some of this important, if essentially supplementary, material will, therefore, be introduced to illustrate our outline of the events themselves.

The outline is presented in loose chronological form, rather than authority by authority. The first reason for this is, of course, that we have sought to conceal as much as possible the identity of the councils we visited and the individuals who were generous enough to grant us confidential interviews. The second reason is that the authorities themselves were not acting in isolation from each other. They may not have been in anything like continuous communication, one with another, but there were various contacts among both officers and members, and at certain key points perceptions of decisions being taken or advice being considered by one authority crucially affected actions in another.

1. Common Labour policy of public transport subsidy

With this potential network of communication in mind, perhaps the factor to note at the outset is that after the County Council elections of May 1981 all six Metropolitan Counties, like the GLC, had working Labour majorities. Moreover, following the Labour Party's annual local government conference held at Blackpool in February 1981, all six Labour groups were committed, again like that on the GLC, to a public transport policy aimed at halting passenger decline and the continual raising of fares by the provision of substantial revenue subsidies funded from local rates. The extent to which this transport policy predominated as the key local issue in Labour's election campaign across the Metropolitan Counties can be clearly seen from the content analysis of election literature carried out by Geoff Lee and Alan Bruce.[5]

The reasoning and the financial arithmetic behind this policy can be appreciated from Table 1 which shows the pattern of passenger subsidies across the six Metropolitan Counties up to and including the 1981-82 financial year:

Table 1

Comparison of total passenger transport subsidies and passenger usage, 1975-76 to 1981-82

	Index of passenger transport subsidy		Index of passenger usage		Index of subsidy on the average domestic ratepayer
	1975-6	1981-2	1975-6	1980-1*	(81-2)
Greater Manchester	100	187	100	77.5	£ 9.46
Merseyside	100	174	100	80.4	£11.53
South Yorkshire	100	461	100	106.8	£25.20
Tyne & Wear	100	414	100	106.8	£15.35
West Midlands	100	122	100	85.4	£ 7.81
West Yorkshire	100	257	100	70.4	£ 7.18

* i.e., before the introduction of the Tyne & Wear Metro system

What this table also shows is that, while a fares subsidy or containment policy might have been something of a novelty in places like Greater London and the West Midlands, this was by no means the case in some of the other Metropolitan Counties. The outstanding example, of course, is South Yorkshire, whose Labour administration had had the ultimate objective of 'free public transport for everyone' ever since its first election to office in 1973. As a preliminary move towards this objective, the council decided first to harmonise fares across the county, which was achieved by January 1976, and then to contain them at a low level. By the time of the May 1981 elections, therefore, fares in South Yorkshire had already been frozen for more than five years, with the result that a two and a half mile bus journey, costing between 20p and 36p in the other Metropolitan Counties, cost just 7p in South Yorkshire. The new Labour administration elected in May 1981 was firmly and more or less unanimously committed to a continuation of this established policy, and as Geoff Lee and Alan Bruce record, it was vigorously, prominently and 'sophisticatedly' defended in the party's election literature:

'1977 pledges were repeated; the fare structure for different mileages in the other five Metropolitan Counties, and Strathclyde tabulated; rateable values explained; the subsidy expressed as a pint of beer a week; costs to ratepayers specified; European experience was shown to prove that South Yorkshire's subsidy policy is in step with the rest of the Western World'.[6]

Tyne & Wear, the other uninterruptedly Labour-controlled metropolitan county, had also had a 'frozen fares policy' since November 1979. But whereas this policy was very much the centre-piece of South Yorkshire's approach to transportation, it had only a secondary role in Tyne & Wear. The council there had pursued since its inception, when it took over the established Tyneside PTE, what could be termed the 'high investment' option, with its development of the Tyne and Wear Metro, first described as 'the first truly comprehensive approach to transport provision in any major British city'.[7] By the time of the 1981 elections the Metro system, substantially financed by central government, had come to dominate both the capital and revenue transport finances of the authority, and obviously constituted an exceedingly powerful qualifying factor to be taken into account by any administration seeking to maintain a cheap fares policy.

The remaining four Metropolitan Counties had all had at least very comfortable Conservative majorities between 1977 and 1981. In two cases - Greater Manchester and West Yorkshire - the incoming Labour groups were committed only to holding fares down - as opposed to increasing them, as the outgoing Conservative administrations were planning. In Merseyside and the West Midlands, though, like the GLC, the local Labour parties fought the 1981 elections on clear manifesto commitments to reduce fares by an average of 25 per cent. The details varied slightly across the three councils - the most significant variation being in Merseyside, where the promise was to 'reduce fares by at least 10 per cent in each year of office', rather than by 25 per cent all at once - but in all three authorities the 'cheap fares' policy was the central feature of the Labour manifesto and in each case it was acknowledged that a supplementary rate precept would be required to finance it.

The first authority actually to implement a policy of fares cuts was the West Midlands M.C.C. In early September 1981, some weeks before either the GLC or Merseyside, bus and rail fares were reduced by an average of approximately 25 per cent and a maximum child's fare of 2p was

introduced. This was followed by Merseyside's 10 per cent
cut on 1st October, the GLC's 'Fares Fair' cuts on 4th
October, and West Yorkshire's introduction of a 30p maximum
off-peak fare for adults on 5th October. Whereas the GLC's
policy necessitated a supplementary rate precept of 11.9p,
the precepts levied by the West Midlands and Merseyside
were 14p and 6p respectively.

2.   The non-issue of legality

The one issue that it did **not** occur to any of the parties
to mention in their election literature, though, and 'what
was conspicious by its absence' in the campaign, was the
question of the **legality** of either the existing subsidies
which the outgoing Conservative county councils intended to
retain or the higher subsidies promised by Labour.[8] This
absence reflected the unanimous prevailing view of the
fares subsidy policy that was recalled for us in our
interviews with both members and officers in the
Metropolitan Counties we visited. It seemed, without
exception, to be seen as an entirely political issue, not a
legal one.

For members, not surprisingly, the fact of their election
on an explicit manifesto pledge was the key consideration.
As one Labour Leader put it:

> 'For generations in local government we understood that
> if you put something in your manifesto and got
> elected, you got on and did it ... Although there were
> cases - such as the **Wednesbury** case [9] - we had
> cherished the belief that people believe in democratic
> government. If you got a popular vote, you could do
> it'.

Officers, equally unsurprisingly, took a slightly more
sceptical view of this 'popular vote', but the potential
illegality of fares subsidies had not apparently occurred
to them either - not even to one County Solicitor who
prided himself on his caution and rigour and on the way he
was 'always on the look-out to protect members':

> 'We believed,in the normal course of events, that this
> was a decision open to the PTA to make. I don't
> think we ever went into it. Legality didn't arise
> .... It was an unusual decision, to reduce fares;
> it was against all the trends and conventional wisdom
> of the day. This sort of thinking was   revolutionary
> in its own way;   it was really going back to
> fundamentals ... So we were conscious that this was
> an unusual decision, but I don't think we went into
> the legal niceties of it in any way at that point in
> time. We thought it was a decision that could be taken
> in the   pursuance of a duty on the authority'.

One of the PTE solicitors we interviewed echoed this interpretation of the law from his more specialist perspective:

> 'No transport lawyer would have doubted the ability of the local authority to subsidise fares, provided it was not done in contravention of the **Prescott** [10] principles. In other words, you didn't just give away free travel, but you had to have regard to what the market would stand in fixing fares. There wasn't necessarily, therefore, an obligation to break even'.

In South Yorkshire, of course, as we have already seen, the idea of subsidised and even 'free travel' was by no means as 'revolutionary' as it appeared to the County Solicitor quoted above. There had been regular and well-publicised council debates over the years, but there is no indication that even the Conservative opponents of the fares containment policy ever thought to question its legality. Their attacks tended to focus on the size of the subsidy and its impact on ratepayers.

If any consideration at all was given to the legality of the policy, it was restricted to an anticipation of some time well in the future, when a dual continuation of a fares freeze and inflation might make the cost of collecting fares more expensive than the revenue they produced. But even at 1980-81 levels of inflation, it would take some years before such a point could be argued to have been reached. In summary, therefore, it would seem that members and officers were as unprepared as each other for the storm that was shortly to be unleashed upon them by the outcome of the **GLC case**.

3. Response to the GLC case

Bromley's challenge to the GLC's precept first reached the courts, as noted above, within a month of the fares reductions coming into operation. As would be expected, the progress of the **GLC case** - from the Divisional Court's initial dismissal of Bromley's application, through the overthrow of that decision in the Court of Appeal, to the unanimous affirmation of that lattter judgment in the House of Lords - was followed with some interest in the Metropolitan Counties. What was quite clear, however, from our interviews with both officers and members in the three Metropolitan Counties we visited, was that the judgment against the GLC in the Court of Appeal and the House of Lords were received with as much surprised by those monitoring the case as they were in the national press.

The lay politician's view was put by the Chairman of a Transportation Committee:

'Not being a lawyer, I virtually took it for granted
that the GLC would come through without any real
problem. And, of course, initially they did. So I
got quite a shock when the Lords' judgment came out'.

The professional lawyer's view, though more cautiously
articulated, was one of almost equal surprise, particularly
at the Lords' judgment. One County Solicitor and Secretary
described how he was:

'surprised that there was no real argument, and that
the judgement had the support of all five Law Lords.
There is **always** room for argument where there is a
discretionary power'. (respondent's emphasis)

Reflecting back to his reactions at the time, the Deputy
County Clerk in one of the other counties we visited felt
that perhaps more consideration should have been paid by
observers like himself to what he termed 'the mood of the
day':

'In some ways I was not surprised, because of the way
in which the GLC had pushed through the decision. I
was a bit surprised, though, at the interpretation of
the 1969 Transport Act.

When a case is brought before the courts, obviously
the case is an argued one, based on legal principles.
But it seems to me that the mood of the day is bound
to influence the judges. You can't prove it, but it's
bound to. And it seems to me that, if you have the
appearance of power being abused, a court will find a
way of accepting the case that's brought against that
authority. And it seemed to me that sort of feeling
was getting through into the decision'.

But if surprise at the outcome of the **GLC case** was more
or less universal, opinions regarding its relevance and
applicability to the transport policies of the Metropolitan
Counties varied considerably, among members and officers
alike. The Transportation Committee Chairman quoted above,
having admitted his immediate state of shock, added:

'But then - maybe out of complacency or optimism - I
still thought, once I did go into it a bit, this
doesn't affect us, because we're under a different
piece of legislation (the Transport Act 1968,
rather than the Transport (London) Act 1969)'.

This too was the substance of **some** of the officer advice
received by members in the immediate aftermath of the
Lords' judgment. As one solicitor recalled:

'I was first formally asked for advice immediately after the Court of Appeal decision. My assessment was that we were acting lawfully. My assessment after the House of Lords' decision was that the position outside Greater London was significantly different in legal terms, and the differences were so significant as to be able to say that the way we had acted in .... was lawful. That was the advice I gave to the Chairman of the Passenger Transport Committee'.

In at least one of the other five counties, though, it was made clear to us that the prevailing legal opinion was far less sanguine and by no means unanimous - with the County Solicitor now taking a significantly different, and more pessimistic, view of the legality of the council's fares subsidy policy than, for example, the PTE Director. As the latter put it to us bluntly:

'[The Secretary] argued we were guilty. I thought not'.

The Metropolitan Counties, therefore, found themselves in a slightly ironical, if not entirely unusual, position. Faced with two sets of unanimous judgments, from the Court of Appeal and the House of Lords, the sheer variety [11] (and, some would argue, the lack of rigour and the superficiality [12]) of the arguments underlying those judgments meant that the Metropolitan Counties were left in a state of almost complete uncertainty as to the legality of their own, essentially similar, fares policies.

4. Approaches to leading counsel

The response of both officers and members to this uncertainty in most, if not all, of the Metropolitan Counties was to seek outside advice - the opinions, usually written, of leading counsel which could reinforce, or in some instances challenge, the advice of the authority's own legal staff.

Some reference to this use of counsel's opinion appeared in the national and local government press at the time. Sir Frank Layfield, QC, for example, was reported as having been consulted by both Greater Manchester and South Yorkshire Councils [13] David Widdicombe, QC and William Glover, QC, by the West Midlands [14] and Merseyside were known to have approached Konrad Schiemann, QC, and Charles Cross. [15]

None of these contemporary reports, however, manage to convey satisfactorily either the nature or the scale that this search for favourable or authoritative counsels' opinion took on in at least some of the authorities we visited. The term 'shopping around' for local advice was mentioned to us on several occasions - sometimes in an attempt to convey an impression of what actually took place in a particular authority, sometimes to emphasise what either did **not**, or should not, take place. For at least most of the elected members involved, however, the very notion that 'shopping around' might produce significantly different interpretations of the same law and thus different opinions would have been an entirely novel one. As one such member cheerfully admitted:

> 'I haven't met a lawyer in my life. I hadn't even bought a house'.

Obviously, not all members were quite as unfamiliar with the legal and judicial worlds as this one. A few, indeed, were solicitors or barristers themselves. In each of the Metropolitan Counties we visited, though, the initial approaches to leading counsel came from the officers. One solicitor, who pointed out that the resulting opinion was both different from his own and substantially less sympathetic to the council's existing fares policy, described how:

> 'The Chief Executive decided (after the House of Lords' judgment) that there was an issue here which was clearly beyond the ordinary compass of officers in this authority to advise on, and that advice from leading counsel should be taken, which it was ....
>
> Unfortunately, the advice received from counsel was that we were likely to be successfully challenged if we didn't fall into line with the GLC decision, in the sense that the interpretation of the 1969 Act could be applied with equal force to the 1968 Act. We therefore had to take account of our economic and financial duty, andthat meant balancing our books as far as was reasonably practicable from the fare box'.

By the time this opinion had been conveyed to elected members, their counterparts on at least one of the Metropolitan Counties **were** actually facing judicial challenge. As early as 18th December, the day following the Lords' judgment, Solihull M.B.C. announced its intention to challenge the legality of the West Midlands M.C.C.'s supplementary rate precept - an action which was confirmed early in January, after advice received from, among others, David Widdicombe, QC, counsel for Bromley in the **GLC case** [16].

Comparable opinions, arguing the essential similarity of the two Transport Acts, are known to have been received at this time (December 1981/January 1982) by several of the Metropolitan Counties. The response of elected members, though, varied substantially, not only from one authority to another, but also within individual Labour groups.

David Blunkett, in his account 'The Road to Cheap Fares' suggests that at least some of the leading members in South Yorkshire took the aggressive and confrontational view that the Chief Executive, in seeking counsel's opinion, was chiefly concerned:

'to protect himself and others, whether politicians liked it or not, and whether it was in the best interests of the community which the local authority existed to serve'. [17]

But even in South Yorkshire, and certainly in the other Labour groups, there were members who were far less staunchly committed to the cheap fares policy - especially in the face of unsupportive legal advice - the possibility or actuality of judicial challenge, and even personal surcharge. One member recalled a Labour Group Executive meeting at which counsel's advice was received and debated:

"I can remember those people who'd always been opposed to it getting up and saying: 'well, that's it, that's the end of that'".

In few, if any, of the Metropolitan Counties, though, did the receipt of a single counsel's opinion actually represent the end of anything. For a start, as the various PTE solicitors we interviewed explained to us, the PTEs saw themselves:

'in a slightly different position to the Council. We had our own fiduciary duty to consider and other things ... we were ... as first cousin to the County Council'.

Another PTE solicitor expanded upon this theme:

'From the PTE angle, there were two important issues. One, fiduciary duty. This was important to us too. We felt that if the County was acting illegally, then we may also be, in accepting the subsidy.

But this was secondary to the **Prescott** case issue. The suggestion that we had to act as prudent businessmen, on business principles, caused us a lot of worry. If this was to be asked of us, this changed the whole situation ... We worked closely with the

43

County, although it was recognised that in the end we would need our own separate advice, because the issues for us were different'.

Here, then, was one potential source of conflicting legal advice for both members and officers. If the county and the PTE were to different leading counsel with even slightly differently emphasised questions or instructions, the resulting opinions would be likely to differ. In at least one of the authorities we visited this was exactly what did happen. The Council had obtained an opinion from counsel which had stressed the distinctions between the 1968 and 1969 Acts, and was thus potentially supportive of its fares subsidy policy and the supplementary precept. The leading counsel instructed by the PTE, however, took a contrary view:

'He told us that the supplementary precept was probably unlawful'.

['What of the distinction between the 1968 and 1969 Acts?']

'He dealt with this. There were differences - the inclusion of town planning, for example. [Counsel for the County Council] made a lot of this. But the advice we received ... was that the differences were not significant enough to alter the Lords' judgment. So the advice was that the precept was void, the subsidy was not lawful, and we were in breach of ordinary business principles in reducing fares".

It was not only officers of the council and the PTE, though, who were earnestly seeking counsel's opinion at this time. Elected members had begun to realise that this was a game that they could play as well, The problem was that most of them had to learn the rules as they went along, and at first even some of the more experienced members tended to tread rather warily. The Chairman of one Transportation Committee recalled how he was more or less forced by his Leader to take personal responsibility for his decision that members should seek counsel's opinion for themselves, independently of the council's officers:

"The Leader said that I had to tell the Chief Executive. 'I'm not telling him', he said. So I have to tell the Chief Exec. that we were going for a second opinion, and a third opinion, if necessary. He'd never had anything like this happen to him in his whole bloody career".

This Chairman's account of ensuing events is, we feel, worth reproducing in some detail, giving an insight as it does into the impact on officer-member relations of members' gradual realisation that they might have a new and exploitable resource at their disposal:

44

"For a start, he [the Chief Executive] said, 'there's no point in going for a second opinion. We've been to ... who is the leading QC in the local government field".

But I'd been told that the thing to do was to go and ask a lot of different QCs until you got an opinion which suited you. But not to get a written opinion - you went and had a chat as it were, and if it wasn't productive, you don't take it any further.

He was totally opposed to this and said so. 'I've got you a QC's opinion. I am your legal adviser, and I'm telling you as your legal adviser that you're outside the law'.

Then I made a mistake, because we got a name on the grapevine ... But he was not a QC, he was a barrister.

And we went down - myself, the Leader, the Treasurer, and the Chief Executive - and we got his opinion. It wasn't as good as we wanted it to be but it was a bit more our way. But then the Treasurer and the Chief Exec. really tore into this bloke and tore him to shreds.

The upshot of this was that I said we must go for another opinion. 'If you say we must go to a QC, we'll go to another QC'. 'You can't **keep** going for opinions', they said.

So we decided to go to ..... who'd given an opinion to [another Metropolitan County], which gave a certain amount of encouragement .... there were certain strands that looked as if they could be developed, and we might get a decent opinion out of it.

I also telephoned [the legal department of a trade union] and they were prepared to finance another legal opinion. Our officers were wary about shopping around for opinions, but ... I was prepared to go to anyone to get legal opinions. And the idea was that if got a good opinion from a QC, we would send the Council officers to that QC".

The senior members on one of the other authorities we visited recounted similar experiences, and recalled the mixed sensations of excitement, apprehension, and frustration that they had felt at the time:

'I kept a diary ... we seemed to be with lawyers every week. I felt very excited, but not knowing how to cope.

We went down umpteen occasions to see Queen's Counsel.
Can you imagine: we were paying these people thousands,
but we were shown into small rooms, skimpy, one cup of
coffee. We sat with our coats on. It was like sitting
with the devil.

We had a long argument with counsel. It was difficult
for us to understand the legal terms ... we were landed
in a totally alien situation. Officers understood ...
but I came out of meetings thinking it was OK then it
was not ... I still had the naive feeling that our
policies were right.

I was 3 or 4 times a week down to London - like a yo-
yo up and down the M1 - to take counsel. We saw two or
three counsel - the officers gave us a list to choose
from, but we chose .... from someone's recommendation in
the party.

But I had the feeling all along that many of the Chief
Officers here were going round the back to advise the
men [the counsel] who were going to advise us. I felt
that the hierarchy of officers here and at the PTE were
not behind us. As good professionals they did it, but
with no enthusiasm.

I felt the gravity of it. People were very worried.
The Leader said it was serious. The implication, the
fear, was surcharge. I was under pressure from my
family, who had heard about the possibility of surcharge
and were against it ... We looked to be on a loser after
Denning'.

5. Judicial challenge

It will be clear from these extracts from our interviews
with both members and officers that **most** of the opinions
received from leading counsel at this time tended to come
against the legality of the cheap fares policies of the
various Labour councils. Even when it was conceded that
there were significant differences between the 1968 and
1969 Acts, there was still the less tangible 'mood of the
day' to be taken into account. One member recalled a
particularly frustrating encounter with one QC:

"I had an argument with ..., arguing that the 1968 Act
was a totally different Act. The requirements for us
were totally different to those for the GLC. I'd read
the wording and it was clear - it gave us the right to
do whatever we felt was in the best interests of the
area from a transport point of view.

46

And in the end he said ... 'OK, you can argue with me
logically and, OK, in logic you are perfectly right -
it is different wording. But the fact of the matter
is that the Law Lords have ruled against the GLC and
they will rule against you'. It added up to him
saying: It doesn't bloody matter what the words say,
you've had it".

But if the emphasis of much of the opinion was similar
from one council to another, what was at stake, at least in
the short term, differed considerably. Being 'on a loser',
in the words of one of the members quoted above, meant
different things on different councils.

The West Midlands members, as we have seen, knew from an
early stage that they were facing a challenge to their
supplementary precept in the courts. Dudley M.D.C. had at
one time shown an interest in combining forces with
Solihull, but the case was eventually brought by Solihull
and the industrialists Guest, Keen & Nettlefords Ltd.
(GKN).

The Merseyside members were also anticipating a challenge
from a local district council - in this case, the then
Liberal-controlled Liverpool City Council.[18] As it turned
out, of course, a case was brought, but by Great Universal
Stores Ltd. (GUS), not by Liverpool.

From West Yorkshire it was reported that Calderdale
M.D.C. investigated the possibility of taking the County to
court.[19] West Yorkshire, though, was not one of the
councils to have levied a supplementary rate, and possibly
for this reason, Calderdale decided not to go ahead.

Tyne and Wear was by the turn of the year in a different
position from the other five counties, for, as part of a
deal linked with government finance for the Metro, the
Council had actually **increased** both bus and Metro fares on
3rd January by some 22 per cent.

The other Labour stronghold, South Yorkshire, was also
unlikely, on political grounds, to face a challenge from a
disaffected district council. It was, however, reported
that the advice the Council had received from Sir Frank
Layfield, QC, was that its policy of fares containment
might also be illegal, and that it might be required to
'repay ratepayers the £53 million a year subsidy which has
been used since 1975', in addition to having to increase
fares by up to 1270 per cent.[20]

Finally, Greater Manchester was also known to have sought
the opinion of Sir Frank Layfield and, whether as a result
of his advice, or whether as a response to unfolding
events, members there took the decision early in February
to raise fares by 15 per cent.

6. The West Midlands case

The principal publicised events that may have played a part at this time in influencing the attitudes and actions of members on other authorities concerned the West Midlands M.C.C. West Midlands, it will be recalled, was the first council to have announced its fares reductions, and also the first to be notified of judicial challenge. It also became the first authority, on 18th January, to announce the abandonment of its cheap fares policy - less than 24 hours **before** Mr Justice Woolf, in an unreported judgment in **R.v. West Midlands County Council, ex p. Solihull Borough Council**, granted applications by Solihull and GKN for orders quashing the County's supplementary precept.

The immediate proximity of these developments led to some confusion and misunderstanding even at the time. It can be established, though, that the legal advice received by members from leading council, and in particular from William Glover, QC, drew attention to the emphasis placed by the Law Lords on the fiduciary duty of a local authority to its ratepayers. [21] On the basis of this and other legal advice received, and with members being warned by senior officers of the likelihood of surcharge and disqualification from office if the court case went against them, the decision was taken at an extraordinary meeting of the Council to increase bus fares by an average of nearly 70 per cent, to abolish the 2p flat fare for passengers aged up to 18, and to postpone the introduction of free travel for the unemployed. The supplementary precept of 14p was thus declared 'null and void' and was reduced to one of 5.75p, reflecting the withdrawal of all financial support for the cheap fares policy.

The following day the Authority sought to argue in the High Court that the policy had not been 'a manifesto gimmick, thought up on the spur of the moment', but part of the policy of the Labour administration of the Council from 1973 to 1977, which had been re-examined in considerable detail and 'at numerous meetings with many organisations' before the 1981 manifesto was prepared. Mr Justice Woolf, however, took the view that such pre-manifesto discussions and deliberations within party groups were insufficient indication of a council having taken properly brought its mind to bear on the issue and having into account 'all relevant matters', and, as noted above, he quashed the Council's supplementary precept that it had itself already decided to abandon.

7. The Merseyside case

Attention now switched to Merseyside, for it was only at this stage, **after** Mr Justice Woolf's judgment in the **West Midlands case** that GUS lodged their application for judicial review seeking an order to quash Merseyside's supplementary precept. The Merseyside Council, it will be remembered, had reduced its fares initially by only 10 per cent, compared to the West Midlands' 25 per cent, and by the time that Mr Justice Hodgson had granted GUS permission to challenge the council's policy, members had already, on 22nd January, taken the decision **against** making the planned future reductions of 10 per cent for the next two years.

In at least these two respects, therefore, Merseyside's case promised to be different from, and arguably stronger than, that of the West Midlands. The case had been brought much later - in fact, some three and a half months after the applicants had received their supplementary rate demand - and it related to proportionately a much smaller increase in fares.

There were, however, other more significant differences as well. One crucial factor which, perhaps because of its technicality, received relatively little publicity at the time, was the respective financial and budgetary circumstances of the two councils. In both the **GLC** and **West Midlands cases** the increased expenditure necessitated by the substantial fares reductions resulted in the loss of Rate Support Grant, in the form of grant holdback. The vagaries of the grant system then in operation, though, meant the scale of grant penalties for which Merseyside might be liable happened to peak at a level below what the council's expenditure would have been even without any fare reductions. Far from losing grant, therefore, the council actually continued to receive at least a small additional percentage grant on the additional expenditure involved in the fares policy.

Relevant as all these considerations were though, it would appear from all published reports of the **Merseyside case** that Mr Justice Woolf attached even more importance to the manner in which the key decisions were taken than to the substance of those decisions. [22] The following brief extracts from the judgment should serve to indicate some of the matters to which the judge paid particular concern. To start with, he drew attention to the differences between the two Transport Acts. Under the 1968 Act, which applies to areas outside Greater London:

> 'It does not automatically follow that the setting of fares at a level which would result in a deficit, which it was practicable to avoid, is unlawful'.

There was discretion to do so, and whether the decision was lawful or not depended on **how** the decision to set the fares at such a level was reached.

The applicants, GUS contended that, as was argued in the **GLC case** the Council only had regard to an election manifesto pledge, and nothing else. But, referring in detail to the affidavit submitted by Councillor Keva Coombes, the Chairman of the Passenger Transport Committee, and, incidentally, himself a solicitor, the judge felt that there was more extensive and "temperate consideration given to the desirability and consequences of 'putting into effect'" the Merseyside policy than there had been in the **GLC** or, presumably, the **West Midlands cases.**

In his affidavit, Keva Coombes claimed that, in recommending the fares reduction to the PTE, he had been influenced by at least nine types of factor, of which the election manifesto pledge was only one. Others had included:

(a) the decline in the number of passengers experienced as a consequence of previous fares increases;

(b) the increasing sense of isolation of many people in the outer areas of the County;

(c) the relatively low level of car ownership in Merseyside;

(d) statements made in the Merseyside Structure Plan;

(e) his view that the 1981-82 Budget, prepared by the previous Conservative administration, had failed to achieve a balance between a proper level of service and revenue;

(f) the state of industrial relations existing amongst employees of the PTE, where there was a history of industrial disputes;

(g) the hardship caused by the high cost of public transport to the sizeable proportion of the County population whose sole source of income is state benefits;

and

(h) the effect that any supplementary precept found to be needed would have particularly on the non-domestic ratepayer compared to the benefits that they may receive, bearing in mind, amongst other things, the extensive effort by way of price-cutting and sales that Central Liverpool Stores were being forced to make at that time to attract people into the City Centre.

The judge concluded that:

'It is not possible to say that the Council did not exercise their discretion properly. In my view there is nothing objectionable in the Council not having considered alternatives, so long as, having properly considered the single proposal, they came to the conclusion that it was a proper proposal to adopt. The fact that a proposal originated in a manifesto does not alter this position.

In the present case it could not be said that the Council had not considered the proposal afresh on its merits after the elections, and no sinister inference could be drawn from the speed with which matters were dealt with'.

In summary, therefore, Mr Justice Woolf found against GUS on all three of their submissions. The county council had **not** misdirected itself in the use of its legal powers; it had **not** acted arbitrarily; and it **had** exercised its discretion in an appropriate manner.

8. Impact of the Merseyside case

Costs were awarded to the county council but, not surprisingly, in view of the uncertainty still surrounding the interpretation of the law, the applicants gave notice that they would seek leave to appeal direct to the House of Lords. In fact, GUS decided, apparently at almost the last possible moment, not to go ahead with an appeal. Several of the people we interviewed, though, and who had been watching the case with close interest, thought that if it had reached the House of Lords, Mr Justice Woolf's judgment would most likely have been reversed. A solicitor, for example, described how he thought that:

'Woolf did a magnificent job in his judgment .... though there were some mistakes in his logic. But we were pleased with the outcome, and when GUS didn't appeal. I am sure the Council would have lost'.

51

The uncertainty persisted, therefore, but the **Merseyside** judgment had at least indicated a way forward, particularly for those councils who had still to come to a final decision on the future of their fares policies. This was especially true for South Yorkshire, where the Labour group had been reported only some three days earlier to be on the point of agreeing to a fares rise of 400 per cent or more.[23]

The South Yorkshire members had, as we saw above, been warned about the likely illegality of their fares policy, which obviously involved a far higher rate of subsidy than that of Merseyside. At the same time, though, they were able now to draw lessons from the way in which Konrad Schiemann, QC, and Stephen Aitchison had successfully presented Merseyside's case. They had been able to demonstrate - to paraphrase both Mr Justice Woolf and the **Wednesbury** principles -that, in choosing to exercise their discretion by subsidising fares, they had given full and proper consideration to all relevant matters, and had not based their decision on matters which were irrelevant. Officers were therefore instructed to produce comprehensive documentation for the Labour group, the Transportation Committee and the full council which would enable it to be fully considered and discussed - the legal situation, the economic and financial situation, the part played by public transport and the fares containment policy in the county's Structure Plan, and especially important, the cost of the policy of both domestic and non-domestic ratepayers. On the basis of this report, the decision was taken to maintain the council's existing policy and not to increase fares.

From the members' point of view, this exercise, at least partially cosmetic though it was, promised to have two major potential benefits. First, if a court case were to be brought against them, they would stand a reasonable chance of winning it; and secondly, even if they lost it, they would be most unlikely to be at risk of personal surcharge.

From the point of view of our research analysis the production of this comprehensive passenger transport review for South Yorkshire members in the immediate aftermath of the **Merseyside case** represented one of the first identifiable changes in the decision-making processes of local authorities brought about as a direct result of the threat of litigation. It constituted an early illustration of the processes of formalisation and bureaucratisation to which we shall return in later sections of the book.

9. Postscript

Far more substantial, and substantive, changes, though, were soon to follow - necessitated by the Transport Act 1983. Between them, the **Bromley** and **Merseyside** decisions still left a considerable degree of uncertainty over the limits of a local authority's power to provide revenue subsidies to public transport undertakings. It was with the professed intention of establishing, in the words of the Secretary of State, 'a clear and consistent legal framework', for the payment of such subsidies that the Transport Act 1983 was introduced.

Its main provision was to require PTEs to prepare an annual plan, covering a three-year period, containing proposals relating to the provision of transport services and the general level and structure of fares to be charged to such services. This plan, having been approved and possibly modified by the PTA, must then be submitted to the Secretary of State and must take into account his/her guidance as to the maximum amount of revenue grants that it would be appropriate for the authority to provide in that year. The Secretary of State, in addition, has the power to determine a protected expenditure level (PEL) for each authority - this 'protection' (from legal challenge) being forfeited both by the authority and by its individual councillors in the event of their deciding on a higher level of subsidy than that considered appropriate by the minister.

With this latter provision particularly in mind, it has been suggested that the Government's objective in this 1983 Act was not so much:

'to resolve legal uncertainities, but rather to exploit them in order to coerce authorities into compliance with the government's guidelines on acceptable levels of revenue support'. [24]

Or, as another commentator put it:

'Revenue support up to a certain level is legal. Expenditure above that level may or may not be. Central government avoids the political problem of being seen to limit revenue support and increase bus fares by leaving the decision to the courts'. [25]

Without in any way refuting this analysis, events since the 1983 Act have in fact taken a slightly different turn. First, none of the authorities which exceeded their PEL in 1983-84 were actually challenged in the courts. And secondly, the Act itself was within a year overtaken by the proposals to abolish the Metropolitan County Councils and the GLC. Following abolition, which took effect on 1st April, 1986, responsibility for public transport in the metropolitan counties has been transferred to joint boards, essentially similar to the PTAs which were in operation before the creation of the Metropolitan County Councils and with which this chapter opened.

Notes

1. Norman Flynn, Steve Leach & Carol Vielba, **Abolition or Reform?** Allen & Unwin, 1985, p. 27.

2. M. Loughlin, **Local Government in the Modern State,** Sweet & Maxwell, 1986, p. 76.

3. (1982) 80 L.G.R. 639.

4. E.g., M. Loughlin, **Local Government, the Law and the Constitution,** The Local Government Legal Society Trust, 1983; M. Loughlin, **op. cit.** n.2, esp. ch. 3.

5. Geoff Lee & Alan Bruce, 'The campaigns and the issues' in S Bristow et al (eds) **The Redundant Counties?** Hesketh, 1984, pp. 106-7, 115-6.

6. **Ibid** p. 115.

7. K Hamilton & S Potter, **Losing Track,** Routledge Kegan Paul, 1985, p. 126.

8. Geoff Lee & Alan Bruce, **op. cit.,** p. 116.

9. A reference to **Associated Provincial Picture House Ltd. v. Wednesbury Corporation** [1948] K.B.223 which laid down the principles according to which the courts would interfere with the exercise of discretionary powers: see chapter six.

10. A reference to **Prescott v. Birmingham Corporation** [1955] Ch.210 which is discussed further in chapter six.

11. See, e.g., Loughlin **op.cit.** n. 2, pp. 69ff; J.A.G. Griffith, **The Politics of the Judiciary,** 3rd ed. Fontana, 1985, esp. pp. 142-9.

12. Loughlin, **op. cit.** n. 2, pp. 73-4; Hugh Stevenson, "Lords' Logic", **The Guardian,** December 19, 1981.

13. E.g., **Local Government Chronicle,** January 22, 1982; **Municipal Journal,** February 5, 1982; **The Guardian,** February 15, 1982.

14. E.g., **The Guardian,** January 8, 1982; **Local Government Chronicle,** January 29, 1982.

15. Stephen Marks, 'Law and Local Authorities: Counsels' Opinion on Budgets and Rents', **Public Money,** June 19, 1982, pp. 49-56.

16. **The Guardian,** January 8, 1982.

17. **Local Government Chronicle**, April 23, 1982, pp. 448-9.

18. **The Guardian**, December 19, 1981; **Sunday Times**, January 19, 1982.

19. **Municipal Journal**, January 22, 1982.

20. **Local Government Chronicle**, January 22, 1982; **The Guardian**, February 15, 1982.

21. See, e.g., **Local Government Chronicle**, January 29, 1982.

22. See, e.g., **The Times**, Law Report, February 18, 1982; **Local Government Chronicle**, February 26, 1982; Loughlin, **op. cit.** n. 2, pp. 76-7.

23. **The Times**, February 15, 1982.

24. Loughlin, **op. cit.** n. 2, p. 80.

25. Chris Skelcher, 'Transportation' in Stewart Ranson et al (eds), **Between Centre and Locality**, Allen & Unwin, 1985, p. 161.

5 Transport in non-Metropolitan Counties

Our research study included two non-Metropolitan Counties, as these authorities also have public transport responsibilities the exercise of which may have been indirectly influenced by the **GLC** and related cases. We also indicated that our choice of non-Metropolitan Counties would be based upon the level of public transport expenditure and would hopefully include one predominantly rural authority.

As a result, included in our sample were two non-Metropolitan Counties, one urban with a high level of public transport revenue support, and one rural with a very low level of support. In order to maintain confidentiality the former is referred to as Urbshire and the latter as Rurshire. These markedly different levels of support reflected sharp differences in policy within the two authorities concerned, the former being a Labour-controlled authority since 1981 with a commitment to low fares and the latter, a Conservative-controlled shire county with a strong commitment to reducing local government expenditure, including severely limiting public transport revenue support and allowing market forces to determine the level of service provided. It would be wrong to draw any general conclusions about public transport in the non-Metropolitan Counties based upon the evidence gathered from these two respondent authorities, and no attempt will be made to do so. External authorities, such as the levels of public transport revenue support and the level of services, including the declining services in the rural areas, do suggest however that these authorities are representative of their type.

Both types of authority have been subject to similar external developments, in terms of the changing policies of

57

the centre, new legislation and 'rules' and the changing economic circumstances already discussed and we make reference to the specific impact of these developments within the two non-Metropolitan Counties we visited, below. In most other respects however, the recent history of public transport in the two authorities concerned, and the role of legal considerations within it, have been so different that they demand separate consideration.

1. Urbshire: The Urban 'High Spender'

This authority has experienced frequent changes of political control in the last 15 years and control changed from Conservative to Labour in 1981. Prior to 1981, the policy on public transport incorporated a modest amount of revenue support, in line with government policy. There was no annual updating for inflation, however, and increases in cost had therefore to be met from increases in fares and/or cuts in services. The incoming Labour administration in 1981 adopted a policy of substantially higher revenue support, with the object initially of keeping fares at the same level and stopping the deterioration in services. As one senior politician from the controlling Labour group pointed out to us, however, the subsidy was not 'huge' and was at the time of the interview (1984) roughly the same as the subsidy provided by the Conservatives would have been had it been inflation-proofed. The public transport subsidy policy from 1981 onwards thus bore close resemblance to the policies adopted over this period by the Metropolian Counties, except that it did not include any **fares cuts** as those of some of the latter authorities did. The Labour Party manifesto had however supported lower fares and the possibiilty of free transport - as a long-term objective.

The essence of the authority's transport policy in the post-1981 period as outlined to us was to arrest the decline in passenger usage and levels of service, which were attributed, at least in part, to the escalation in fares. The intention was to improve personal mobility in an area with a low level of car ownership and 'appalling social deprivation' judged by other social indicators. The effect of the policy adopted was to raise the subsidy per head to a level which was still much lower than the lowest Metropolitan County, and it was therefore felt by the controlling group that such a policy maintained the necessary balance between transport users and rate payers. It was therefore considered to be consistent with the authority's fiduciary duty to the latter.

One striking feature in this authority, which is reasonable to assume is present in other urban non-Metropolitan Counties, is the complexity involved in public transport planning, when compared to the Metropolitan Counties. This is largely attributable to the absence of a Passenger Transport Executive, responsible for all or most

of the operations within the area. The result of this was
that the authority had to bring together the district
councils who were operators, the private operators, British
Rail, the trade unions and other interested parties. The
authority's approach to this was to encourage operators to
enter into Agency Agreements, for which there were
precedents, and to propose the establishment of a joint
Transport Committee of operators and the county council,
for which there was none. The object in both cases was to
improve the structure of public transport and the decision-
making framework, to promote the integration of services
and to avoid a wasteful competition and overlap of routes.
However, the authority failed to obtain the agreement of
all parties on these proposals, despite offering, as an
inducement, to forego their control on fare and service
levels as a condition of granting subsidies. As a result,
the authority turned to Co-ordination Agreements as a
method by which integration could be improved even though
this would do nothing to improve the structure of public
transport. However, there were problems here as well. It
became clear that binding agreements not to compete would
fall foul of Restrictive Practices Law and this prevented
operators from co-operating. In the event, therefore, the
authority had to rely on operators to co-ordinate in
practice without legal agreement and this had happened in
some areas.

In common with the three Metropolitan Counties we
included in our sample, this authority had not considered
that the policy of higher subsidies adopted after the 1981
election raised any legal difficulties. It had been
assumed that the authority had the power to provide higher
subsidies being a matter within its legitimate discretion.
The **GLC case** case had, however, alerted the authority to
the possibility that this might not be so. However,
initial advice from within the authority had been that the
GLC case could be distinguished on the basis, **inter alia**,
that they derived their powers from different legislation
(the Transport Act 1968) and that their policy had not
involved cuts in fares. As a result, counsel's advice had
not been obtained at this stage and the only external imput
had come from the Association of County Councils who had on
the authority's request, obtained some general advice from
the Department of Transport which 'did not take the matter
any further'. However, the Highways and Transport
Committee ultimately resolved to obtain counsel's opinion,
because members were worried about the position, having
heard of the possibility of a legal challenge from local
industry. As a senior officer put it to us, this was done
"as a form of insurance - an insurance option".

Counsel's advice had been favourable - pointing in
particular to the differences in the legislation under
which the authority derived its powers, and this had
removed much of the anxiety. There had been several
possibilities of a challenge to the supplementary precept

from two businesses and the local CBI. However, one of the businesses went into receivership, the other was stopped by its head office and the CBI-backed challenge did not materialise.

In subsequent years, the higher subsidy policy has been retained. However, there have been no fares reductions it being 'difficult enough' to avoid increases because of the cost of the subsidy and the potential rate support grant penalty implication. It had, however, been these financial considerations, rather than doubts about legality, which had mitigated against fares reductions, although the authority did consider that its fiduciary duty to ratepayers would be a factor if such a policy were to be considered. Fares remained, therefore, at their 1981 level apart from the introduction of a zoning scheme and a 4 per cent increase which had been built into this in 1984.

2.   Rurshire: The Rural 'Low Spender'

This predominantly rural authority has been under Conservative control throughout its history and the post 1981 period, on which this research is focused, merely saw a continuation of a policy on public transport which had been adopted in the mid-seventies. To understand developments over the last few years, it is therefore necessary to examine briefly the history of this policy.

The policy originated in a Transport Committee decision in 1975 to set a budget limit on public transport revenue support of £150,000 for each of the three years from 1975-77 inclusive. The significance of this decision becomes clear when one realises that the 1974 budget had been for £250,000 and the provisional figure for 1975 had been £400,000. It was precipitated by the authority's concern about the rapidly escalating cost of revenue support, coupled with the belief that existing policy was unduly restrictive of car users in urban areas. However, this seeingly straightforward switch in policy reflected an underlying ideologically inspired belief that the authority's approach to transport planning was misconceived. The result was that the decision also involved major changes in the way the authority determined how revenue support would be allocated. Transport planning prior to 1975 was described to us thus:

> 'We were rational and objective, we measured everything, absolutely. Rooms were full of information. The transport co-ordinators ... tended towards intervention planning: review network, define need, adjust provision.'

Thus, the authority assessed needs, determined the nature and level of services required and then subsidised the operators to enable the service to be provided. Under the policy adopted in 1975, this approach was scrapped.

60

Instead, operators were required to identify commercial services and those which were uneconomic and, until they did so, no subsidy was to be paid. Once this had been done, parish councils, (chosen as appropriate representatives of rural and village communities), were asked to say what services they wished to have, over and above the commercial one offered by the operators. The authority then considered these requests and decided which services to 'buy back' by offering revenue support to the operator providing the best tender. Much of the traditional work of the authority's planners in the transport field, therefore, became redundant. There was no longer any objective measure of needs or network planning and the only monitoring of services was by an annual survey, designed simply to establish that the service was in fact running. These changes were reflected in the structure of transport management within the authority. A split was made between the Engineers' Department and the Planning Department, those responsible for public transport being assigned to the latter. This was seen as appropriate by those involved in transport co-ordination, one of whom commented that:

> 'an engineer's concern is to quantify everything. Our concern is qualitative and subjective. They would want objectively to establish aims, review needs, service provision etc. This objective planning obscures the essentially subjective judgments embodied in the criteria which define planning.'

Officers involved in transport planning informed us that this policy switch had not led to a dramatic drop in services and that there had been surprise at what operators were willing to provide as well as doubts about whether the previous levels of revenue support had been necessary or justified. As the policy developed however, it did not meet with the approval of Government, for although the centre was anxious to curtail the amount spent nationally on public transport revenue support, particularly in some of the metropolitan counties, it was also concerned about maintaining adequate levels of service in the rural areas. In the late 1970s, the authority therefore came in for some forthright criticism from ministers at the Department of Transport for the low level of its bid for Transport Supplementary Grant (TSG) and its failure to spend even at its TSG levels or at a level which provided the same support from year to year, in real terms. This criticism had no impact on the policy, however, and ultimately in 1978-9 the centre attempted to penalise the Authority by accepting only 6% of its bid for Capital Resources under TSG. For a number of reasons however, this had little effect on the authority's finances and, given the controlling groups attitude to public expenditure - both local and national - it was not a penalty which was likely to induce any significant change in public transport policy and nor did it.

It is important to see this authority's policy on public transport revenue support, as part of a wider transportation policy. Officers pointed out that the authority had been at the forefront of experimentation in transport provision, in looking for alternatives to buses and in pressing for a relaxation in restrictions on non-conventional provision. They were anxious to claim credit for recent legislation in this direction since the 1979 General Election. In this respect, as in others, the authority's policy placed great reliance on the market to provide a service, that is, if there was a demand they provided a service.

As intimated above, the authority's transport policy, and in particular its policy on revenue support continued unchanged into the 1980s and is now well established. The budget limit on expenditure for 'buying in' services has been raised and was running in 1983-4 at approximately £230,000 per annum. However, this figure is tiny when compared to most authorities with transport responsibilities, and in real terms, it is substantially less than even the £150,000 annually imposed at the inception of the policy in 1975. The strategy now used to implement this policy has four stages. Operators declare which services they intend to withdraw (as uneconomic), the authority decides which services will be 'bought back', parishes are then given the opportunity to express their views and finally, buying decisions are adjusted to take account of these views. It was emphatically asserted to us by more than one officer involved, that the Committee's decision on what to 'buy back' and officers' recommendations, were based upon the 'high Tory strategy of buying off trouble' - in this case from the parish councils which 'shout the most'. This approach was defended, however, on the basis that it recognised the subjective political decisions involved in transport planning and was responsive to expressed demand which was preferable to assessing need. As one officer put it:

'our policy is simple: we buy services from operators. We are brokers, mediators between supply and demand. We do not try to define, shape, or stimulate demand. It is a naive approach to ask people if they want a service - they would say yes. ... it is a market mechanism policy.'

Politically, the leader of the authority would go further than the current policy does. He regards no subsidy and no local authority role as the best option, whilst favouring the retention of a local discretion to intervene and offer support. His view is that the free market will provide and will rationalise evenly and avoid distortion. 'It would be like food and clothes - the best markets in the world' he remarked 'where what is offered is what is demanded'.

Numerous variables mean that it is difficult to assess the impact that this policy has had on the overall level of service within the authority and perhaps more important, on the mobility of people, particularly in the rural areas. It is the belief of transportation officers that the network is much the same as it was 10 years ago, but, the interesting point is that, given the policy, they just do not know. They argue, however, that operators have been reasonable in what they say is uneconomic and in the price they offer to provide a service for, and have become more efficient. Equally, parish councils have been reasonable in the services which they request and often accepted service cuts or suggested reductions, so much so that the budget - particularly in the first five years of the policy, had been underspent. What is unclear, however, is how reliable the views of parish councils are as to the real level of demand for services in rural areas. Reservations were expressed by some officers and members on this. It is also worth pointing out that the policy has been the subject of continued criticism from opposition parties, as well as district councils under Labour control, for its perceived failure to meet needs in both urban and rural areas.

Within the authority's Transportation Department, the policy is popular with officers despite the limited role it creates for them. It was we were told, clear and easy and made for a 'comfortable existence'. It also had the merit of separating the issues, particularly the subjective political decisions and social responsibilities from commercial and financial considerations.

Given the extremely modest level of revenue support, it is inconceivable that the legality of the authority's policy would have been challenged on the basis that it had exceeded its statutory powers or breached its fiduciary duty to ratepayers, by spending too much. It is not surprising therefore that the **GLC case**, and the subsequent fares cases, had no real impact within the authority. Both within the Solicitor's Department and elsewhere, there was little awareness of the cases and they were not generally seen as being in any way relevant to the authority. Indirectly, however, the **low** level of revenue support did raise questions about legality and in particular about whether the authority was complying with its statutory obligations. For, although there was no specific obligation on the authority to provide **any** subsidy for public transport, under section 2 of the Transport Act 1978 they were required, **inter alia** to produce an annual public passenger transport plan containing:

'a review of the county's needs, and the needs of communities comprised in it, in respect of public passenger transport services, and the extent to which those needs are met by existing services (this review

63

to be accompanied by an account of the criteria applied to determine need).[1]

Thus, whilst all those in the authority we spoke to were confident that the low level of subsidy itself could not be successfully challenged, some openly expressed the view that needs were not assessed or reviewed and that this made the authority vulnerable to legal challenge. This matter had however been reviewed by the Solicitor's Department at the inception of the policy and they had advised that, if the council consulted with parish councils, then this would suffice. Since then the controlling group has consistently maintained that, by inviting parishes to request services, they **were** reviewing and assessing need. This assertion has been regularly challenged by opposition groups on a political level, most notably in 1981, when four opposition Labour county councillors produced an alternative public passenger transport plan in which they drew specific attention to what they saw as the authority's failure to comply with the provisions in section 2 of the Transport Act 1978 referred to above. However, there is no evidence that any group opposed to the policy actually levelled the charge of illegality against the authority and no legal challenge was mounted. One of the opposition councillors involved in the 1981 alternative plan told us that this was because no one had the financial resources to go to the courts and, because it was felt that even if a challenge were successfully made, the authority would simply assess need and then opt not to provide it. These comments highlighted the fact that, whilst significant, the legal uncertainty here was in no way comparable to that surrounding the transport policies of the Metropolitan Counties following the **GLC case.** Thus, although there may have been some doubt about the means used (or not used) to arrive at their policy, there was no dispute about the legality of the broad thrust of what this authority was doing.

Note

1. Sub-section (2) (a). Non-Metropolitan Counties were
    also under a duty 'to develop policies which (would)
    promote the provision of a co-ordinated and efficient
    system of public passenger transport to meet the
    county's needs ...' (section 1(1)(a)(i)) and had power
    to 'make grants towards any costs incurred by persons
    carrying on a public passenger transport undertaking'
    (section 1(5)).

PART III
ANALYSES

6 On legal process

1. Developments in substantive administrative law relating to local government

We turn now to the developments in the substance of Administrative Law relating to local government which have been occasioned by the public transport fares cases, in order to examine the impact they have had within the authorities in our sample, both in the transport field and in relation to other functions. Consistent with the conventional Administrative Law categories, [1] these developments can most conveniently be analysed under two headings: firstly the natures and extent of the local authority statutory powers and duties and secondly, the exercise of statutory discretionary power and the question of abuse of power.

(a) Statutory powers and duties:

At the centre of developments here has been the nature and extent of the powers of the GLC and the Metropolitan Counties to subsidise public transport, under the Transport (London) Act 1969 in the case of the former and the Transport Act 1968, in relation to the Metropolitan authorities.

(i) The **GLC case**: The House of Lords' interpretation of the GLC and LTE's powers under the Transport (London) Act 1969, has been exhaustively analysed and debated elsewhere and we do not propose to repeat that analysis here. [2] An outline of their powers, as interpreted by the House of Lords, is however necessary.

Under section 1 of the 1969 Act, the GLC were placed under a duty:

'... to develop policies and encourage, organise and
where appropriate, carry out measures which (would)
promote the provision of integrated, efficient and
economic transport facilities and services for Greater
London.'

The LTE's general duty, contained in section 5, was:

'... with due regard to efficiency, economy and safety
of operation, to provide ... such public passenger
transport services as best meet the needs for the time
being of Greater London.'

Under section 3 the GLC were given power to make grants
to the LTE 'for any purpose'.

Each of these powers were examined by one or more judges
in the House of Lords (or Court of Appeal, with subsequent
House of Lords approval), with the emphasis being placed on
the significance of the words 'economic' and 'economy' in
sections 1 and 5 respectively, and on the implicit limits
such words impose on the powers, including the subsidy
power of the GLC under section 3.[3]

The 'paramount subsection'[4] for the House of Lords was,
however section 7(3) which set out the financial duties of
the LTE. Section 7(3) provided, in part that:

'The Executive shall so perform their functions as to
ensure so far as practicable:
(a) that at the end of each ... [accounting] ... period
... the aggregate of the net balance of the
consolidated revenue account ... and ... the general
reserve of the Executive is such (not being a deficit)
as may be approved by the Council ..., and
(b) that if at the end of any accounting period of the
Executive the said aggregate shows a deficit, the
amount properly available to meet charges to revenue
account of the Executive ... in the next following
accounting period of the Executive exceeds those
charges by at least the amount of that deficit.'

This provision was originally examined by Lord Justice
Oliver, in the Court of Appeal, but his comments were
broadly approved by the House of Lords (Lord Diplock
excepted). He dismissed the suggestion that this sub-
section was merely an accounting provision. He interpreted
it as a 'break even' provision imposing an obligation on
the LTE to operate on ordinary business principles and to
try, as far as practicable, to cover operating costs from
fare revenue. In arriving at this interpretation, heavy
reliance was placed on the earlier case of **Prescott v.
Birmingham Corporation**[5] which was said to have established
the principle that public transport undertakings should
operate on ordinary business principles unless the relevant
statute expressly provided otherwise.[6] The effect of this

interpretation of section 7(3) was that the GLC, who were[7]
obliged to have regard to these obligations on the LTE,
could only make grants in aid of revenue as a necessity to
make up unavoidable deficits, rather than 'as an object of
social policy'. It had therefore been beyond the powers of
the GLC under the 1969 Act to make the grants to the LTE
which had enabled the 25 per cent cut in fares to be
implemented.

As we noted in chapter three, the reaction of GLC
officers and members to this approach to the interpretation
of the 1969 Act was one of considerable shock and dismay.
This was not an emotional response to the fact that the
ruling had gone against them since it was clear that at
least some of the officers had recognised the possible
vulnerability of the fares policy to challenge (albeit in
their view unfairly) on the ground of unreasonableness
(which, of course, had been the original basis of the
action brought by Bromley). This awareness did not,
however, prepare them for a decision that seemed to be
saying that the Act did not empower them to make a grant in
aid of a particular transport policy at all. Such a
decision was viewed as incomprehensible because it bore no
relationship to the policy that they had understood to have
been embodied in the 1969 Act. For one officer the
interpretation, first adopted following the intervention of
Lord Justice Oliver in the Court of Appeal, was an 'Alice
in Wonderland' construction totally at variance with the
'self-evident' structure of the Act. In effect, it
appeared to transform what the GLC officers and members
believed to be a provision concerning the LTE's financial
management into one which precluded any serious influence
on the part of the GLC over public transport policy in
London, despite the terms of the duty set out in section 1.
The ruling, therefore, ran completely counter to the view
that the 1969 Act had represented a major change in public
administration in the transport field, making the ordinary
business principles presumption derived from **Prescott v.
Birmingham Corporation** totally inappropriate.

The social role of public transport had been fully
addressed in argument before the House of Lords (the GLC
having been effectively wrong-footed in the Court of
Appeal) and it was certainly tenable, at the very least, to
hold the view that this would be a legitimate reason for
making a grant to LTE. Indeed the GLC and its counsel were
confident that this was the correct interpretation of their
statutory powers and believed that they had every prospect
of persuading the House of Lords of the correctness of
their view. In the event Lord Diplock in the House of
Lords **was** prepared to consider that the 'needs of Greater
London' referred to in section 5:

'may be better met by a public transport passenger
service that falls far short of paying its own way than
by one that does pay its own way.'[8]

71

He had, therefore, no difficulty in accepting the use of the grant power for a social purpose (but not in the instant case for quite discrete reasons). This approach did not, however, seem to make any headway with the majority in the House of Lords. They preferred a range of variants on the stringent economic approach taken by Lord Justice Oliver. The discrepancy in the constructions given to the words used in the Act is a demonstration of the scope for choice that can be left to the courts when it comes to determining Parliament's intent in framing a particular provision. Certainly the construction that prevailed in the courts was not one that was incontrovertibly dictated by the terms of the Act itself as there was no specific limit on the apparently broad power in section 3(1) to make grants 'for any purpose'. Insofar as any limit must have been intended the most obvious source would be section 1 which specifies the GLC's role in the provision of public transport in London. The adoption of a much more restrictive interpretation of the grant power is nonetheless explicable in terms of judicial technique. Since there was nothing in the Act which specifically required socially-motivated grants - unlike the express duties imposed on local authorities in, for example, the Housing Acts - and by legal tradition the courts are denied access to the parliamentary debates concerning the enactment of legislation as a guide to its interpretation, an 'established understanding' about how public transport was to be run would readily be accepted as controlling the provisions to be construed.

The 'understanding' selected by the House of Lords was the 'ordinary business principles' presumption. It is questionable, however, whether this presumption was established prior to the **GLC case** as a general principle. Close scrutiny of the judgments in **Prescott v. Birmingham Corporation,** which was the primary authority relied upon, does not support the existence of any general principle that public transport should operate on 'ordinary business principles'. The **Prescott** case was, rather, concerned with the interpretation of particular statutory provisions (very different from these found in the 1969 Act) which were **themselves** regarded as imposing this obligation. The readiness of the House of Lords in the **GLC case** to seize on this aspect of the judgments and treat it as establishing a general principle cannot, therefore, easily be justified in doctrinal terms.[9] We will, therefore, return to this issue when developing our 'explanatory model' in chapter eight.

The construction in fact adopted by the House of Lords was not absolutely preclusive of socially-motivated grants, for, although their ruling was in sufficiently forceful terms for the officers of the GLC to doubt that it had any such power, it was still open to receiving a more indulgent gloss from the Divisional Court in the GLC's subsequent action for a declaration against the LTE.

By adopting an interpretation so contrary to the
understanding of those working under the Act, the decision
in the **GLC case** had the effect of creating caution and
uncertainty about all the powers on which the GLC relied.
Officers no longer had confidence in their own judgments
about the meaning of statutory provisions and one officer
told us he thought that they would need to seek advice on
an extensive scale to see how **a court** might interpret the
statutory language. This certainly seems to have been the
case as reports and advice to committees thereafter often
included specific advice on statutory powers, in many
instances prepared with the assistance of counsel as well
as the GLC's own legal staff. This advice was seen as
particularly important in relation to the 'grey areas' in
the powers used to support the increased range of
activities in which local government had by then become
involved. Although advice about how a court was likely to
interpret a particular statutory provision was sought as a
necessity, the experience of the **GLC case** meant that it was
not held in high esteem. One officer doubted the ability
of the courts to deal with the issues involved in statutes
such as the Transport (London) Act 1969 because of their:

> 'inability to judge policy issues about which they were
> not informed.'

This view, which is also applicable to predictions by
counsel as to future court behaviour, was echoed later in
public by the then Comptroller of Finance at the GLC.[10]
The authority was, however, compelled to accept this
constraint on its powers.

Nonetheless it is interesting to note that, whilst the
immediate impact of the House of Lords' interpretation was
to create considerable uncertainty, in the longer term it
has, in the opinion of senior officers, led to a greater
willingness to extend the range of activities to the
boundaries of the authority's statutory powers - often
relying on legal advice based upon a close scrutiny of the
statutory provisions concerned. The GLC were perhaps
alerted to the possibilities of this approach, and
encouraged to adopt it themselves, by the threat of legal
action from the London Borough of Camden. The Borough
alleged that, following a 100 per cent fares increase in
the wake of the House of Lords' decision, the GLC was now
in breach of its obligations under section 1 of the 1969
Transport Act to 'promote the provision of integrated,
efficient and economic transport facilities and services in
Greater London'. This threat, perhaps more than anything
else, demonstrated that the law had potential as a resource
to facilitate activities, as well as to prevent or
constrain them, an issue which we return to in our
concluding analysis.

Many lawyers would themselves quibble with the House of
Lords' interpretation of the 1969 Act, purely as an

exercise in statutory interpretation. The reaction to it within the GLC, however, illustrates problems which are more fundamental and far reaching in their implications. On one level, they display a degree of ignorance about the canons of statutory interpretation and the role of the courts in it, and about the declared unwillingness of courts to become involved in the merits of decision-making. More importantly however, they raise questions about whether the existing approach of courts to statutory interpretation and to the review of administrative decision-making is appropriate and beneficial to good public administration. Moreover, even if it is or could be made so, the question arises as to whether judicial review itself is an effective or appropriate method of controlling and supervising the exercise of statutory power, whilst giving effect to administrative requirements. This is an issue which we return to later in the analysis.

(ii) Reactions in the Metropolitan Counties: As we recorded in chapter four there were equally surprised reactions to the House of Lords' interpretation of the GLC's statutory powers, in the Metropolitan Counties. The solicitor and secretary of one PTE summed up a view which was widely expressed when he said:

> 'No transport lawyer would have doubted the ability of the local authority to subsidise fares provided it was not done in contravention of the **Prescott** principles. In other words, you couldn't just give away free travel, but you had to have regard to what the market would stand in fixing fares. There wasn't necessarily therefore an obligation to break even. Everyone was absolutely shocked and astonished by the **GLC** case.'

The Metropolitan Counties derived their statutory powers from the Transport Act 1968, rather than the Transport (London) Act 1969. The House of Lords' interpretation of the latter Act in the **GLC case**, was not therefore conclusive as to the extent of the Metropolitan Counties powers of subsidy, but it did produce a similar lack of confidence in the accepted interpretation of the scope of their own powers. Two sections of the 1968 Act were of particular relevance. Under section 9(1) both the Metropolitan Counties and the PTEs were under the same general duty to exercise and perform their functions:

> ' ... As to secure or promote the provision of a properly integrated and efficient system of public passenger transport to meet the needs of that area with due regard to the town planning and traffic and parking policies of the councils of the constituent areas and to economy and safety of operation; ... '

The financial duty of PTEs was set out in section 11. It read in part:

'The Executive ... shall so perform their functions ...
as to ensure so far as practicable that the cumulative
net balance of the consolidated revenue account of the
Executive ... does not show a deficit at the end of any
accounting period of the Executive after taking into
account any amount which, at the date when that period
ends, has been specified in a notice under s.13(3) of
this Act in respect of expenditure incurred before that
date but has not yet been received by the Executive.'[11]

As can be seen, these provisions bore a close resemblance
to those found in the 1969 Act. The issue upon which legal
attention was therefore focussed was whether the courts
would be likely to interpret the 1968 Act in a similar way,
or whether the differences which did exist between the
Acts, meant that the Metropolitan Counties' powers of
subsidy were wider. Potentially relevent differences were,
firstly, the fact that the general duties imposed on
Metropolitan Counties and PTEs under section 9 of the 1968
Act set out above, were wider than those imposed on the GLC
and LTE. In particular, there was the duty to have:

'due regard to the town planning and traffic and
parking policies of the councils of the constituent
areas.'

Secondly, this general duty on PTEs was **not** made
expressly subject to their financial duties not to incur
deficits, as it was in the case of the LTE. Further, it
will be seen that the financial duties themselves were, in
some respects, less onerous than those imposed on the LTE
in the 1969 Act. Finally, as noted earlier the GLC's
general duty included promoting 'economic' transport
services. The 1968 Act imposed no such requirement on
Metropolitan Counties who were only required to have due
regard to 'economy and safety of operation'.

These differences were, therefore, subjected to close
scrutiny, initially by the Metropolitan Counties and PTEs'
own lawyers in an effort to see whether it was possible to
escape the straightjacket of the ordinary business
principles presumption and grant subsidies, if not as an
object of social policy, then at least in circumstances
other than where it was a necessity. The uncertainty
generated by the House of Lords' unexpected construction of
the provisions of the 1969 Act had, however, created
considerable difficulties in statutory interpretation and
all judgements were, therefore, necessarily tentative. The
legal advice which emerged within the three Metropolitan
Counties in our sample, was that these differences between
the 1969 and 1968 Acts **were** sufficient. The solicitor of
one of the PTEs however, took a different view. In view of
the seriousness of the situation, and the fact that several
Metropolitan Counties faced the possibility of legal
challenge, all but one of the six took the advice of
leading counsel. The PTE's in the three authorities in our

75

sample did likewise. This produced mixed results. The balance of opinion was in favour of the differences between the Acts being sufficient. As is well known however, South Yorkshire was advised otherwise, as was its PTE, and the position was further complicated by the fact that the advice given to another Metropolitan County's PTE was unfavourable, thus conflicting with the opinion of that authority's own Counsel. This latter conflict led to strains in the relationship between the authority and the PTE, and could have resulted in court action, had it not been for the outcome of the **Merseyside case.**[12] Overall, however, the most significant feature of all the conflicts in advice received by the Metropolitan Counties and their PTEs, was the fact that they related to the construction of the 1968 Transport Act itself, and could not, therefore, be explained by the differing levels of subsidy between Counties, or the reasonableness in legal terms, of the policies adopted in each authority. The fact that there was conflict on the nature and extent of Metropolitan Counties, and PTE's powers under the 1968 Act, demonstrates clearly the legal uncertainty which had been generated by the **GLC case.**

It is interesting to note that while 'in house' advice in the Metropolitan Counties was united, the opinions of their counsel differed. The 'in house' view owed something to an opinion expressed by lawyers in more than one authority, that the House of Lords had been influenced in its interpretation of the 1969 Act by the highly controversial political image of the GLC and its leadership, and the publicity this had created. Here are two comments which illustrate this:

'... It seems to be that the mood of the day is bound to influence the judges. You can't prove it, but its bound to. And it seems to be if you have the appearance of power being abused, a court will find a way of accepting the case that's brought against that authority and it seemed to me that sort of feeling was getting through into the decision.'

and:

'The Lords were influenced by the Livingstone issue - Red Ken, revoluntionary socialist change. A scare had been building up in the press. The Lords may have felt they had to intervene.'

There was also a widely held view that the **GLC case** represented the 'high water mark' of court intervention, and that any subsequent cases were likely to reflect this. This was of course, a view which was to be borne out by later developments, both in relation to the 1969 Act itself, in the **GLC v. LTE**[13] case, and in relation to the Tranport Act 1968 in the **Merseyside case.** (It should be noted in passing here that in GKN's challenge to the West

76

Midlands County Council's fares policy, the question of differences between the 1968 and 1969 Acts was not argued, the council pre-empting this by resolving to abandon the policy.) It is equally important to note, however, that neither the **GLC v. LTE** case nor the **Merseyside case** was appealed and they are only Divisional Court decisions. One senior solicitor was strongly of the view that, had the **Merseyside case** been appealed, it would have been reversed in the Court of Appeal and that the Divisional Court decision was a 'climb down'[14] in particular, because it had decided that the financial duties and the general duties on PTEs under the Act were equal, and that one did not dominate the other. His view was that the Court of Appeal would have judged the former to override the latter, as the House of Lords had decided it did in relation to the LTE under the 1969 Act.

Despite these qualifications, there is no doubt, however, that the two Divisional Court decisions did restore some order and certainty to the interpretation of the statutory powers of Metropolitan Counties in this area. Equally, there remained a sense of unease which probably led to a more cautious approach to exercising their statutory powers, particularly the power of subsidy.

One final point of interest is that the question of the power and duties of the authorities under the 1968 Act had arisen in one Metropolitan County prior to the **GLC case** and the 1981 elections. Here, the outgoing Conservative administration had been proposing fares increases and service cuts, but it had been put to them by the solicitor to the PTE that their policy may be in breach of their statutory duties under section 9(3) of the Transport Act 1968 to 'secure or promote the provision of a properly integrated and efficient system of public passenger transport to meet the needs of the area'. The results of the election however, meant that the issue was not taken any further.

(iii) <u>Impact in non-Metropolitan County Councils</u>: It is not possible for us to assess the impact of the House of Lords' interpretation of the 1969 Act on non-Metropolitan County Councils, only two of which were amongst our respondent authorities. However, bearing in mind that these councils have a different structure for public transport and operate under wholly different powers of subsidy,[15] the relevance of this part of the House of Lords' judgement in the **GLC case** (as distinct from the question of reasonableness and in particular fiduciary duty) was likely to be more marginal. However, Urbshire, the predominantly urban county council within our sample with high levels of subsidy, did take counsel's opinion on their policy.

Not surprisingly, we detected no impact in Rurshire, the predominantly rural and very low subsidy county we visited.

In this authority however, a question about the interpretation of its statutory powers and duties had arisen concerning the meaning of the obligation on it, under section 2(2) of the Transport Act 1978, to review public transport 'needs'.

(b) Abuse of power

The primary ground which the supplementary precept issued by the GLC was held to be unlawful turned, as we have shown, on the construction of the 1969 Act. However, the decisions of the appellate courts highlighted aspects of the decision-making by the councils which were regarded as an abuse of power and would have been sufficient to establish the invalidity of the precept. These were the apparently rigid adherence to the manifesto commitment concerning fares and the approach thus taken to decision-making as well as the failure to take account of the Council's fiduciary duty to its ratepayers.

(i) The manifesto and the decision-making process: In declaring unlawful the decision of the GLC to reduce fares in accordance with the terms of their manifesto, the appellate courts were not relying on any new principles of law, although the actual decision definitely came as a shock to local authorities everywhere. The underlying principle is that a discretion must be exercised properly and this means that nothing, whether a policy, a contract or a manifesto commitment, should operate so as to close the mind of an authority at the time that the decision is being taken. This does not mean that a manifesto commitment is irrelevant. On the contrary, it is a matter which the authority should take into account and to which it is entitled to give great weight. It must, however, be examined alongside all other relevant considerations.

Despite this well-established principle, the courts have traditionally been reluctant to interfere with local authority decisions taken in accordance with their election promises. Recognising the political nature of local authority decision-making and the elected status of councillors, juges have tended instead to assume compliance with this principle of lawful decision-making, in the absence of strong evidence to the contrary.[16] The decision of the Court of Appeal and House of Lords that the GLC had, in breach of this principle, fettered their discretion by a slavish appearance to their election manifesto, was seen by some as a departure from this practice. The tone of some of the judgments (being as they were, out of keeping with some earlier judicial pronouncements on manifestos)[17], undoubtedly lent support to this view. Others recognised, however, the importance, which the court had attached to the speed at which the GLC had sought to implement its manifesto commitment, and the way in which this had left the council open to the charge that it had not taken account of other relevant considerations, not least the

78

financial costs. The view on this, however, was that, whilst such a charge could be made, it could not be substantiated. GLC officials were at pains to point out that proper attention had been given to all the relevant considerations, including the financial ones. There was a feeling therefore, that the court's objection was really to the **weight** which had been given to the competing considerations (even though this is properly a matter exclusively for the local authority to determine) rather than to any failure to **consider** all relevant matters. Of relevance here, was the importance attached to the manifesto promise, as opposed to the financial interests of ratepayers. Whatever the truth of these assertions, it is clear that the courts were greatly aided in coming to the conclusion they did by the constant assertions of senior members of the controlling Labour group that they were 'bound' by the election manifesto to implement the 25 per cent cut in fares, as well as by the speed of implementation. Taken at face value, this all pointed to ill-considered and fettered decision-making. What some felt was needed in order to assess this evidence more accurately, but which was conspicuously absent in the courts, was an awareness and an appreciation of the political context in which such decision-making occurs. Specifically, one had to be sensitive to the political debate within the Labour Party about the extent to which previous Labour-controlled councils had failed to implement manifesto promises, and the importance which the incoming Labour members on the GLC had attached, both before and after the election, to carrying out their manifesto promises. Only then could one appreciate that the statements by Labour councillors to the effect that they were bound by manifesto promises, were examples of political rhetoric rather than fettered discretion, and that they reflected the importance which was being legitimately given to the manifesto, as one of the relevant considerations to which they were to have regard.

On the question of the speed at which the policy had been implemented, it was necessary to appreciate, as a matter of fact and political reality, that the options for public transport fares policy and the relevant considerations, had been exhaustively debated and analysed before the 1981 election had ever taken place. This debate had taken place within the major political parties in London and within the GLC and LTE. Indeed, the latter is rumoured to have had a 'red plan' and a 'blue plan' ready for implementation, according to which political party won the election. The decision-making process had therefore begun long before the elections took place.

From a local government perspective, it was, therefore, somewhat artificial to concentrate exclusively on the formal procedures of the GLC, after the election, in order to test whether all relevant matters had been considered, and that no irrelevant items had been brought into play.

This raises wider questions about the legal, as distinct from political, status of manifestos and political parties and whether it is realistic and appropriate for the courts to demand the degree of deliberation by a local authority before a decision is taken, which would have been appropriate had the members not considered any change in circumstances, (such as the grant penalty implications), it would be unrealistic to expect that they would start with a blank sheet in deciding on their public transport fares policy. Decision-makers cannot be expected to forget all the arguments and discussions to which they had been party before the election, and to abandon the views and positions which they had adopted, in order to be re-persuaded, or persuaded to take a different view. Consequently, the debate at committees and in the council chamber after the election, was bound to be less detailed and more speedy than if the matter was entirely new to those involved.

The finding against the GLC on the manifesto was, of course, disasterous for them but it was also crucial in the decision of the West Midlands to give up the fight against a challenge to its low fares policy. As one officer put it:

'They couldn't demonstrate the consideration of all relevant factors ... He missed the manifesto point.'

Thus illustrating that this application of a well-established principle had caught them unawares because it seemed normal practice for a council to act in the way that the West Midlands had done. Catastrophe did not, however, befall the third authority, Merseyside, to be challenged on the legality of its transport policy which involved the implementation of a manifesto commitment. In that case there was a finding that the manifesto had not been blindly implemented following an exploration of the process by which the council's policy had been adopted. For many of the authorities interviewed this success was seen more as a matter of presentation than substance. As an officer of the West Midlands PTE observed:

'I think the [West Midlands County] Council did have a planning context - The Passenger Transport Executive only had to be satisfied that there was a proper reason - the council's mistake was to say that it was in accordance with the manifesto. They told this to Merseyside ... who then stage-managed everything - meetings - there were more debates - the idea that fares should relate to the price of petrol and the damage to the community etc.'

This almost cynical view of what happened was not confirmed by Merseyside but it was clear from all the authorities interviewed that considerably more attention is now being paid to the **way** decisions are being taken even though this may not actually mean the decisions reached are any different; the presentation of the processes of decision-making has become a high priority. Thus most of the authorities interviewed emphasised the steps that they had taken to ensure that it appeared that they had in fact taken account of the relevant consideration:

'We were also reminded that rather than producing reports which would enable us to get the results we wanted from members, we had a duty to spell things out in detail for their own protection.'

'There were long debates in council - they hadn't worked this way before, it had all been decided in caucuses and not in full council. There were long boring debates ... they were constructing a debate ... rather than to have a pre-considered idea ... they had to be seen to be constructing policies within the council ... they couldn't be seen to decide outside the council.'

'In the current budget all transport proposals were discussed and justifications demanded - we needed to say we had gone through the process.'

'There is a greater caution in what we say in writing a report to committee - should items be public or private.'

'Reports were now brought together and duplicated in some cases from one committee meeting and the next, that is, whereas in the past all the same reports would come before the committee at different times in the year, the tendency now would be to put the report in again when the decision had to be taken so that it could be said that all of the matters in the report had been considered at the decision-making meeting.'

We return to some of these themes later in the analysis.

There appeared to be some inconsistency between the refusal of the officer in one authority to accept that they were simply going through the motions:

'it is not just a matter of one line on a word-processor.'

and the view of most members and officers interviewed that it was a matter of presentation. What was clear, however, was that it was felt by almost everyone that the relevant considerations were nearly always being taken into account. In other words, they believed that they had generally complied with the legal standard but the previous practice of local government meant that it was not always possible to **demonstrate** this in a court of law. Every effort was now being taken to ensure that in future this would not be a problem.

Although the substance of decisions does not, therefore, seem to have been affected by the increased emphasis on observing procedural standards, at least one authority felt that it does afford even greater protection should they wish to be more adventurous in the use of their powers:

'Before, when you were faced with something that seemed on the face of it to be unreasonable, you didn't tend to take it further. That was before we were in the position of almost ritualistically putting down all the factors. Now, if you go to one of the leading politicians, they can do it almost automatically.'

To this extent the emphasis on presentation faced in all authorities following the **GLC case** has been a boon.

(ii) <u>Fiduciary duty</u>: We discuss fiduciary duty here, under the broad heading of abuse of power, in the belief that this duty is rightly seen as a 'relevant consideration' to be taken into account when exercising discretionary powers. We are reinforced in this view by subsequent cases to the **GLC case** which have considered the duty, in particular the case of **Pickwell v. Camden L.B.C.**[18] where Mr Justice Forbes and Lord Justice Ormrod, clearly saw the duty in this light. The latter commented that:

'the exercise of this duty ... [is] ... a relevant factor to be taken into account in determining the ambit of statutory powers of discretion.'

But that it would not be right to regard fiduciary duty as opening:

'a route by which the courts can investigate and, if though appropriate, interfere with any exercise of discretionary powers by local authorities.'[19]

Dicta of this kind[20] seem to make it clear that it is wrong to see fiduciary duty as standing apart from the principles laid down in **Associated Provincial Picture Houses Ltd v. Wednesbury Corporation**[21] and operating as an overriding consideration dictating a certain course of action which, if it is not followed, will automatically render a decision unlawful. Rather, as a relevant consideration, it is something which must be taken into account but which does not assume paramount importance, except in the rare case in which to treat it otherwise would be to act so unreasonably that no reasonable authority could have acted that way (i.e., the **Wednesbury** test of unreasonableness).

Since its 'resurrection' in the **GLC case**, the meaning of fiduciary duty has been extensively discussed,[22] and its origins traced,[23] and it is unnecessary for us to engage in analysis of this kind here. It is sufficient to note the words of Lord Justice Jenkins in **Prescott v. Birmingham Corporation**, where he said that:

> 'the local authorities are not, of course, trustees for their ratepayers but they do owe an analogous fiduciary duty to their ratepayers in relation to the application of funds contributed by the latter.'[24]

Fiduciary duty featured in the House of Lords decision in the **GLC case**, in two distinct but connected ways. Firstly, expressly or by implication, the concept influenced four of the five Lords (Lord Diplock excepted) in their interpretation of the GLC and LTE's statutory power and in their finding that the latter was obliged to operate, as far as possible on ordinary business principles. This was either because the provisions of the Act had to be interpreted in a way which was consistent with the GLC's fiduciary duty, or that the duty was reflected in the provisions themselves, particularly those which imposed the financial duties and constraints on the LTE, and indirectly therefore, the GLC. In either case, by breaching its fiduciary duty, the GLC was seen as having exceeded its statutory powers. The reasoning here owed much to the **Prescott** case and the words of Lord Justice Jenkins, quoted above.

Secondly, and independently of the GLC's statutory powers under the 1969 Act, Lord Diplock (who held that the GLC was in any event **intra vires** its powers), supported to some extent by the comments of other Lords, concluded that the GLC was in breach of its fiduciary duty to its ratepayers because, **inter alia**, it had failed to maintain the necessary 'balance' between them and transport users. The main factor here was that central government grant penalties had the effect of nearly doubling the cost of the fares policy to the ratepayer - leading Lord Diplock to speak of a:

> 'thriftless use of ratepayers' money and a deliberate failure to deploy to the best advantage the full financial resources available to it by avoiding any action that would involve forfeiting grants from central government funds.'[25]

In his judgment, this thriftlessness amounted to such a clear breach of fiduciary duty that it was (fortunately he remarked) unnecessary for him to decide at what point a breach of fiducary duty normally occurred. Of the various dicta on the subject of fiducary duty, it was these comments of Lord Diplock which were to prove the most controversial and problematic for local authorities. This was largely because he was not content simply to regard the duty as a relevant matter which the decision-maker is obliged to consider but which he may, subject to the resulting decision not being totally unreasonable, give as much or as little weight to as he sees fit. Instead, relying on **Prescott v. Birmingham Corporation** and on **Roberts v. Hopwood**[26], Lord Diplock treated the duty as a separate and distinct test or standard with which local authorities have to comply, independent of the **Wednesbury** principles.

Thus, in his judgment, not only had the court to be satisfied that the financial interests of ratepayers had been considered. The judges had also to decide whether, in their opinion, sufficient weight had been to given to those interests to comply with the local authority's fiduciary duty - itself a judicially created and defined concept. This is clear from Lord Diplock's comments referred to above, to the effect that it was unnecessary for him to decide **in the instant case** at what point a breach of fiduciary duty normally occurred, thus conceding that in other cases it would be necessary and proper to do this.

<u>Reactions in the GLC</u>: As we have already noted, at least one senior officer within the GLC had formed the view that the authority may have been vulnerable to challenge on the basis of fiduciary duty, bearing in mind the extra cost created by grant penalties. He had not, however, spoken out at the time. Despite this, the scope and importance which the House of Lords, particularly Lord Diplock, attached to fiduciary duty came as a surprise to both officers and members at the GLC and created considerable alarm. Concern centred on the overriding character with which fiduciary duty appeared to have become endowed, and the uncertainty involved in having the courts decided from case to case whether the duty had been complied with or not. This alarm was greatly exacerbated by the terms in which Lord Diplock chose to present his judgment. Thus, whilst he may have thought it fortunate that the GLC's breach of fiduciary duty was so clear that it was unnecessary for him to decided at which point such a breach normally occurred, the GLC (and many other local authorities), took a very different view. For them, his failure to spell out at what point a breach would occur, made the uncertainty problem acute. Furthermore, his reference, to a:

> 'deliberate failure to deploy to **the best advantage** the full financial resources available to it'

paved the way for the argument that any expenditure over and above the necessary to fulfil minimum statutory obligations, might be regarded as a breach of fiduciary duty. Finally, the words immediately following -

> 'by avoiding **any** action which would involve forfeiting grants from central government funds'

strongly suggested that, at least in Lord Diplock's view, **any** expenditure decision involving loss of Rate Support

Grant would, almost automatically, involve a breach of the fiduciary duty owed to ratepayers.[27]

The alarm which all this generated in the GLC and in local authority circles generally, is reflected in an talk given soon after the case by Maurice Stonefrost.[28] He criticised the House of Lords for making fiduciary duty an overriding consideration of a binding character rather than just a relevant consideration to be taken into account. He was also critical of the way the duty was implied into and blurred with the construction of the statute. The effect of the House of Lords' judgment, he argued, was not so problematic in extreme cases - including the **GLC case** itself, given the double cost to the ratepayers arising from grant penalties. There were also some activities which it was clear would not constitute a breach of the duty. Where the House of Lords' judgment did create serious problems and uncertainties, however, was in 'grey areas' where no real guidance is offered. This, he felt, was likely to result in a tendency for legal challenges to be made and to the danger that the courts become the decision-makers. In this way fiduciary duty became, in his words, 'whatever a particular court decides it is'. Thus, whilst fiduciary duty before the **GLC case** was, at most, a 'long stop' whose main value was its existence rather than its use, he feared that it would be seen as much more than just a reminder of this kind.

In particular, he expressed his worry that some now see it as a tool to hold in check public expenditure and taxation with which they disagree. Stonefrost saw these developments as bad for the law and the judiciary itself. His main concern, however, was about its effect within local authorities. Fiduciary duty now appears on reports and agendas. Officers are faced with the difficulty of being asked to advise whether a particular course of action would involve a breach or not. Yes or no answers are required but the matter is really a question of opinion which it is for the council's members to decide. Further if officers do advise that the action under consideration might be a breach, then this would weigh very heavily in any subsequent challenge. Ultimately, resort may be had to counsel to decide on the question of fiduciary duty, which again gives rise to the danger that judgments which are properly a matter for elected members are made instead by barristers.

Strong support for this proposition comes from one QC advising the GLC, in the wake of the **GLC case**. He was asked what rate increase would be possible whilst still complying with the council's fiduciary duty. He told us that he nearly gave a figure, but didn't because the GLC would then have gone for this and he would have become the 'dictator of London' when he was not a representative with any direct knowledge. Instead, he confined himself to saying that the figure the GLC had in mind was beyond the dividing line, whilst declining to say where that line was. Other counsel have not, however, been so restrained and it is known[29] that opinion has been sought and given on, for example, the levels of rents and school meals charges which would be lawful, and those which would be in breach of fiduciary duty, leading one commentator to remark that:

'it is difficult to imagine a more clear-cut example of the legalisation of political issues.'[30]

Stonefrost's analysis is that of an administrator, conscious of the practical effects of a legal judgment on administrative and decision-making processes and his views on this aspect of the House of Lords' judgment in the **GLC case** may not be shared by all Administrative Lawyers. There will be those, for example, who were trained in the wake of decisions like **Roberts v. Hopwood** and **Prescott v. Birmingham Corporation** who would take as their starting point the assumption that fiduciary duty **is** an overriding consideration and that the courts have rightly taken it upon themselves to judge what that duty is and whether it had been breached in a given set of circumstancs. This assumption is less likely to be acceptable, however, to Administrative Lawyers schooled on the idea that the court will not substitute its own judgment on policy matters for that of the local authority or other body charged with the exercise of discretionary power. Whether, as some lawyers have argued,[31] the House of Lords' judgment does represent the partial abandonment of this principle of non-interference in the merits of local authority decisions, or whether this is a mis-interpretation is, in the present context, of secondary importance. What **is** important is that a senior administrator in local government, and no doubt many others like him, interpreted the House of Lords' judgment as offending against this principle, thus producing profound uncertainties and difficulties for the decision-making processes of local government. In other words, the perception that the courts were willing to intervene in local authority decision-making in this way has the same effect, whether or not it was accurate. It means that political judgments become legal judgments made by local government lawyers, counsel and ultimately, in some cases, the courts.

Reactions in the Metropolitan and non-Metropolian Counties: It was readily conceded by solicitors in all the authorities in our sample that, prior to the **GLC case**, fiduciary duty was not an issue or a term used within their authority. This is not to say that the impact of policy decisions on ratepayers received no consideration, or that decision making processes and procedures did not, to a greater or lesser extent, ensure that such matters were taken into account. This was not seen however, as a distinct legal duty upon local authorities.

Despite this relative unfamiliarity with the concept of fiduciary duty, it would be wrong to describe reactions to this aspect of the **GLC case** as being universally ones of either shock or surprise. Rather, the reaction varied so markedly from authority to authority, and as between officers, members and counsel that it is difficult to make any generalisations. If any pattern emerged at all, it was in terms of the major impact it had on members and the comparatively modest one it had on officers, particularly the lawyers, and counsel. However, there were exceptions to these generalisations, as well as marked divergences of opinion between different authorities. These differences cannot be attributed entirely to uncertainties generated by the House of Lords judgments. Inevitably, reactions to the fiduciary duty aspect of the case were influenced by the bearing they had on the particular circumstances of each authority.

Taking the solicitors within the three Metropolitan Counties in our sample and the solicitors to Urbshire, there was an wide agreement amongst them that fiduciary duty was not an issue, or was not the main issue, in their authority. There was also agreement that the duty had been overstated, and was correctly seen as 'part of the overall concept of reasonableness' or as a 'relevant consideration' and nothing more. One solicitor to a Metropolitan County left us in no doubt however that he regarded the duty as a valuable one. He commented that he saw this aspect of the **GLC case** as:

> 'a timely re-statement ... of the law ... the duty of elected members to ratepayers as trustees, the duty to keep balance between receivers and payers.'

In particular, he saw Lord Diplock's judgment as introducing the:

> 'comparatively new concept of thriftlessness in relation to the use of resources',

which had arisen, he thought, because of the need to have regard to grant penalities as a relevant consideration or, as an adjunct to the relevant consideration of fiduciary duty. More than one solicitor also voiced concern that, whilst he was satisfied that proper consideration had been given to ratepayers, committee minutes and other documentary evidence may not have been sufficiently comprehensive to make this easy to prove.

Counsel's opinion in two of the three Metropolitan Counties in our sample confirmed the solicitors judgment. In one Metropolitan County, however, their counsel took a very different view. He considered that the authority concerned had failed to consider the effects of their fares policy on ratepayers and the fact that a highly significant effect of that policy was that the council would incur greater grant penalties, which would increase the burden on the ratepayer.

As intimated above, the reaction of members in Urbshire and the Metropolitan Counties in our sample was very different. As one officer put it fiduciary duty 'got banded about as **the** big issue'. The following are the words of the chairman, and then the deputy chair, of the Transportation Committee in one of the Metropolitan Counties:

> 'We knew about **Wednesbury**, but we had not really understood the gravity of what it meant. This fiduciary duty was the main element.'

> 'Fiduciary duty was the most favoured word here for 12 months - balancing our spending for passengers against the general good of the ratepayers. We had not worked on our fiduciary duty.'

The interesting thing about these two comments and a number of others we heard, is that they suggest that fiduciary duty may, in the minds of members, have become synonymous with what is really, in Administrative Law terms, the **'Wednesbury** principles' and the whole concept of abuse of power. If this is true, then it can probably be traced back to the judgment of Lord Diplock in the **GLC case**, discussed earlier. The interpretation of this judgment articulated by Stonefrost, is one which was undoubtedly shared by many members and it is not surprising that the importance this placed on fiduciary duty should lead to it being seen as, at least, the key element in the concept of abuse of power. What is also interesting is how enduring the importance attached by members to the issue of fiduciary duty has been. One solicitor told us that, although he did not mention it, members remembered it and continued to refer to it. Another solicitor commented that:

> 'issues like fiduciary duty are now before the committees and in the minds of members on a day to day basis'

in his particular authority, documents on fiduciary duty had been prepared before committees by the Treasurer. Bearing in mind the general alarm which the fiduciary duty concept generated amongst members, perhaps the most surprising reaction we encountered was from the chairman of the Transport Committee in the Urbshire. He was very aware of fiduciary duty, and had a well formulated and impressive defence of the Council's policies if challenged. Perceptively, however, he commented that the duty:

> 'tends to be thrown in as a relevant consideration, but its really just a hurdle to get over - it hasn't stopped anything.'

An alternative view was put to us by a QC who has advised one of the counties in our sample since the **GLC case**. He saw fiduciary duty as being the area in which the **GLC case** had had the biggest impact. His assertion was that, with examples being given of the effects on typical ratepayers of alternative spending decisions, members did now think about the rate consequences of their actions. He added by way of example that:

'a 4 per cent increase could be what break the camel's back or at least it can lead to an investment decision'

such as a firm going outside an otherwise desirable local authority area, to a neighbouring authority with lower rating, but where access to the former is still good.

Since the **GLC case**, as indicated at the beginning of this section of our report, much has been done by the courts in the **Merseyside case** and in other cases such as **Pickwell v. Camden L.B.C.**, to narrow the scope which fiduciary duty appeared to have taken on following the House of Lords judgment. Not surprisingly, these developments have been recognised by solicitors and counsel, though less so by members. One solicitor said, for example, that following later cases like **Camden,** fiduciary duty is 'something which is of relatively minor importance as a concept in itself'. Similarly, a QC advising the GLC commented that developments since the **GLC case**, the **Camden case** in particular, had diminished its impact so that **'Roberts v. Hopwood** is now cloistered'. In his view the court didn't want to get involved in value judgments and in this sense, the **Camden case** had been a 'non-starter'. After the immediate impact, the effects of the House of Lords' 'resurrection' of the fiduciary duty concept, seem to have diminished, and court decisions, at least at Divisional Court level, suggest that in this area, as in others, the **GLC case** was a 'highwater mark'. The lasting impact of this aspect of the House of Lords' judgment should not, however, be underestimated. There is no doubt that it has led to major changes in the decision-making processes of some local authorities, with more information and advice being given to committees and explicit references being made to the considerations, including fiduciary duty, which had been taken into account in making decisions. This has been demonstrated above. The rebirth of fiduciary duty has also had a surprising effect on the attitudes of members, albeit that these attitudes may be based upon certain misapprehensions about its scope and meaning. We return to some of the issues later in our analysis.

2. Developments arising out of local authority involvement with the legal process

We turn from the substance of Administrative Law and the constraints that it imposes on local authorities to more general observations arising out of their involvement with the legal process. Here three issues are considered: the attitudes of local authorities to judicial review as a means of ensuring that they observe the limits on their powers; the problems affecting standing to challenge local authority decisions; and the impact that the increased resort to counsel's opinion is having on local authority decision-making.

(a) Attitudes to judicial review

It is apparent from our study that the process of judicial review - the way in which Bromley was able to mount its challenge to the GLC's supplementary precept and fares policy - is regarded as unsatisfactory by many members and officers. This should not be surprising in view of the fact that, as has been seen, the **GLC** and subsequent cases seemed to change local authorities' understanding of both the literal terms of the governing legislation for public transport and of the appropriate ground rules for the conduct of much local government business. However, the dissatisfaction did not arise simply because precepts had actually been held to be unlawful and future plans were inhibited. It stemmed from unease with the process rather than a repudiation of the existence of limits of their powers; such limits were acknowledged by those we interviewed, albeit more readily by officers than members. The unease was partly with the way the process works - primarily a technical matter - and partly because it was considered that the decisions involved were not suitable ones for judges to take.

At the technical level there were three main concerns, apart from the question of standing which is discussed separately below, namely: the uncertainty of the process; the impossibility of doing justice to local government procedures; and the effect of the adversarial system on the way in which issues are ventilated.

Although the authorities are not unused to litigation their experience in recent years has been more as a plaintiff or prosecutor than as an actual or potential defendant. This may have left them unprepared for the experience of the years under review. Unquestionably they found the process very uncertain. Of particular concern was the way in which the legal issues can shift as a case goes through the various court levels. Thus in the **GLC case** itself there was undoubted confidence in the arguments that had to be met in the Divisional Court and success there confirmed the council's own perceptions of the law. At the appellate stage they found the whole basis of the case had shifted, primarily as a result of the intervention of the judges hearing the case and the decision was unexpectedly against them. The possibility of this being repeated undoubtedly lay behind the fear expressed in Merseyside that an appeal against the unsuccessful challenge to their fares policy might well have been successful. Uncertainty was also a factor in the West Midlands County Council deciding not to fight the challenge to their transport policy. After the event there was clearly a feeling that the decision concerning their policy could well have been favourable if it had been brought before the courts after the **Merseyside case** and not immediately after the **GLC case**. The outcome of cases was thus viewed as partly dependent on the haphazard order in which challenges arise and the West Midlands County Council was not prepared to take the risk of a fight given the mood prevailing immediately after the **GLC case**.

Nor does uncertainty for those involved in a case cease once the outcome is known. As the saga of events after the GLC case demonstrates, the requirements of a decision may well be open to quite different constructions. This was a problem both for the GLC and the LTE in deciding what, if any, subsidy it could give or receive; their respective advisors reached quite opposite conclusions about the possibility of reducing fares from the high levels introduced immediately after the House of Lords' ruling. Similar difficulties were faced by the other authorities who were concerned about the relevance of the underlying principles of the decision to the conduct of their own affairs. Even when an authority resorts to judicial review itself in order to resolve an issue, as the GLC did in relation to its Direction to the LTE over fares at the end of 1982, a favourable outcome is not definitive for all interested parties. The GLC's action against the Executive only resolved the legality of a subsidy and a reduction of fares as between themselves, it did not mean that a separate challenge by a ratepayer or the auditor would not have been successful. In particular, the action did not resolve the question of whether the subsidy was consistent with the GLC's fiduciary duty.

A second complaint about the process of judicial review was that in the experience of many of those interviewed it was not possible to do justice to the way in which local government operated. This was in part a criticism of the level of understanding that judges have of the ways of local government, but it was also a manifestation of the feeling that there were problems of proving to a court that the legal standards for decision-making had actually been observed. Certainly many of the authorities felt exposed to the possibility of challenge after the **GLC case** because they did not have 'on the record' an examination of all the relevant considerations before a decision about transport subsidy had been taken. This was not because there had necessarily been a failure to take them into account but

because there had never seemed to be any need to make a
formal reference to them. Since the **GLC case** there has
undoubtedly been an increase in formality but it is seen by
and large as a matter of form and not substance:

> 'We are now setting down many things that were
> previously implicitly understood.'

Specifically, when policy decisions fall to be made by
committees, the tendency is now for members to be deluged
with paper on all aspects of the subject in order to be
able to demonstrate later that all the relevant matters
were before them. In most cases, these papers had
previously been before the committee for consideration and
decision, and the practice in the past would have been to
assume to present them again was unnecessary. Having
previously considered them, the members could be taken to
be seized of their contents and their relevance to the
policy decision to be taken. Similarly, special papers of
more general considerations relevant to decision-making,
are now prepared and put before committees when policy
decisions are to be taken. Previously, whilst members
could reasonably have been expected to take such matters
into consideration, their relevance may not have been
expressly highlighted or referred to in debate. One
obvious example here is the local authority's fiduciary
duty to its ratepayers, which has been the subject of
papers to committee members in a number of authorities.
Finally, when resolutions are drafted and decisions taken,
effort is now made to list or make express reference to all
the considerations which have been taken into account by,
for example, using expressions like 'having regard to' or
'bearing in mind' x, y and z, 'the Committee resolved to
...' etc. The concern in each case is to ensure that, in
future, they will be in able to defend successfully the
legality of their decisions, should they be challenged.

The third source of dissatisfaction with the process of
judicial review is that its adversarial nature has a
restrictive effect on the legal issues addressed in any
given case. This view is by no means an original criticism
of civil litigation but it is particularly pertinent in the
context of local government decision-making since many
parties may be interested in the outcome but only the legal
arguments of some of them are brought before the court.
Thus decisions about transport subsidies will be of concern
to the authority making the grant, the transport operator,
local authorities contributing to the funds of the grant
authority and central government as well as the ratepayers
and the auditor and perceptions about the legality of a
decision by one of these may well be affected by the view
taken of another's actions. For example, in the **GLC case**
the proposed grant penalties were a big factor in the
decisions of the Court of Appeal and the House of Lords but
their legality was not in question. Yet if the penalties
were unlawful the GLC's grant might not have seemed so

thriftless. Of course, the decision to impose those penalties could itself have been challenged by the GLC but this was regarded as unrealistic in the context of the action brought against it by Bromley. Similarly the concession by West Midlands County Council that the reduction in fares proposed in 1981 was unlawful made the willingness of the West Midlands PTE to fight the proceedings brought against it seem untenable. In the Executive's view the council did have a planning context which would have justified the reduction in fares. However, it considered that the Council had made the mistake of saying that the reduction was in accordance with its manifesto and was, therefore, seen to be doing the right thing for the wrong reasons. The nature of the process is thus seen as confining the context in which the decision under attack is taken. These criticisms do not, however, go to the heart of the process itself and there was a strong feeling on the part of many officers and members that it was entirely inappropriate for judges to have been in any way involved in determining the size of the subsidies given to public transport.

This was partly because it seemed to them that political decisions were being taken by people who were quite unaccountable. The most vehement expression of this view was a member's statement that:

'The judges were class-ridden ... vandals in ermine.'

But the underlying attitude of opposition was shared by members of both Conservative and Labour authorities. As one member of the former said:

'The courts should not have interfered; the electorate should have taken charge.'

It was partly because the judges were seen as unqualified in terms of their expertise, access to information and knowledge of the mechanics of local government. More fundamentally, however, there was a feeling that judical review tended to impose a **judicial** framework on local government decision-making. It was as if the courts wanted to remould local authority decision-making in the image of their own processes, and hold that anything which departs from this is unlawful. Thus, within the constraints of the limited knowledge and expertise of the judges about both the issues and about local government in general, and within the limited time available, the courts review the legality of a decision by taking a very small selection of what they regard as **the** relevant or irrelevant considerations. These are then tested against what is know of how the actual decision was made. To officers and members in local government, this tends to be seen as a quite unrealistic exercise, because it fails to take account of both the variety and complexity of counter-veiling **political** decision-making in local government. It is also seen as ignoring the period of time over which policies emerged and are developed and implemented. This point is well illustrated by the **GLC case** where, despite the overall responsibility of the GLC to develop policies which promoted 'the provision of integrated, efficient and economic transport facilities and services for Greater London', and its many other statutory powers and duties which had a bearing on the transport issue, the House of Lords boiled down the issues, relevant or irrelevant, basically to the interests of passenger transport users, the interests of ratepayers and the manifesto promises. Thus, all the other relevant considerations concerning transport planning in London, like road usage, repair and building, commercial and private vechicle usage, parking, environmental issues - such as air and noise pollution, were almost completely ignored. This was despite the fact that they had all clearly and legitimately played a part in the development of the 'Fares Fair' policy for public transport, over a long period.

The implications of judging the legality of local authority decision-making in the context of this judicial framework, extends far beyond the individual case. It is not just that a particular local authority might find that it is judged according to a framework which is alien to it, and which bears no relation to the reality of its own decision-making process. Even more significant is that, in an effort to insulate themselves from successful legal challenge, local authorities will rely increasingly on legal advice from within and outside, about the view a court might take of the issue. The effect of this will be greatly to increase the influence of lawyers and, indirectly, the courts over decision-making. This will be at the expense ironically, of exactly what, it is claimed, the law seeks to achieve, namely a proper consideration of all the issues.

As one officer critic put it:

> 'I simply don't think it is a matter for one, two or three people to purport to make these sort of judgments. If this isn't a just once in ten years process and it is well based in law and precedent, then Administrative Law becomes another tier of executive government, either explicitly or implicitly, by counsel's interpretation of what he thinks the judges will decide on certain issues.'

These criticisms, which are given added weight by the increased use of counsel's opinion we discuss below, raise important issues for Administrative Lawyers which it would be unwise to simply dismiss as the partial views of persons unwilling to accept legal constraints on their powers. Undoubtedly, and understandably, the position of officers and particularly members of local authorities means that, in their enthusiasm to carry out their functions effectively, they sometimes display an ambivalent attitude to the demands of the law. As we have noted, however, both officers and members were often quick to highlight their own awareness of, and support for, the limits on their powers. This probably owes as much to bureaucratic convenience, as to their awareness of the dangers of granting wide powers, unrestrained by law. It should not be overlooked that the certainty provided by a clear legal framework can be as much a benefit to the administration and to the decision-maker, as to those on the receiving end of local authority actions. It was largely for this reason, rather than out of distain for legal controls, that the decision in the **GLC case** and the uncertainty it created was so severely criticised.

Severe criticism did not, however, lead to much in the way of constructive suggestions as to how the process of judicial review could be modified so as to avoid these problems, whilst continuing to fulfil the desired function of imposing limits on the powers of the local authorities. There is much work to be done here both by Administrative Lawyers and by public administrators, if improvements are to be made.[32] What all are agreed on, however, is that all those engaged in the review of decision-making should be sensitive to the practicalities of administration and management and that this quality is lacking amongst the judiciary.

(b) Problems of standing

Although the question of the legality of public transport subsidies has been a matter of considerable concern both within and without local authorities, the number of challenges to reach the courts has been restricted to three, namely, those involving the GLC, Merseyside and the West Midlands. Moreover, although the **GLC case** seemed to open up the possibility of challenges in relation to other matters there have, as yet, been relatively few. A major explanation for this must be the apparent drawing back from the full rigour of what the **GLC case** was actually thought to decide (exemplified in the GLC's own action against the LTE) and the increased use of legal advice to avoid further challenges, but important factors are also the difficulties facing many of those who might wish to challenge the legality of a local authority decision.

The requirement of a 'sufficient interest' (or standing) in order to bring an application for judicial review means that local government decisions cannot be challenged by just anyone. There are, however, a wide range of people and bodies who do have the requisite standing. In the context of public transport subsidies they would include the transport operators, contributing local authorities and their ratepayers, local politicians and, of course, the auditor. The existence of standing does not mean that an action will actually be brought and there are a number of reasons why some who legally are in a position to act do not do so. The transport operators interviewed certainly expressed doubts about the legality of action proposed by the local authorities and the LTE, following the **GLC case**, would only implement subsequent directions once they had been approved by a court of law. In most instances, however, there seemed to be an attitude that it was not sensible to test every arguable point. It must, after all, be remembered that they are in a working relationship with the authority and this would undoubtedly be harmed if they were continually in court. Moreover, their working relationship seems to enable them to resolve many legal problems well before litigation would even be envisaged. Ratepayers are a more likely source of challenge, assuming they are aware of their rights, given the financial burden that an increased or supplementary precept will impose and after the **GLC case** the threat of action by them was the most common to be referred to by local authorities. However, a challenge will itself require costs to be incurred and it is notable that those that have actually materialised or have been taken seriously were those which emanated from large commercial businesses or had the backing of bodies such as the CBI. In one area a challenge collapsed with the bankrupcy of the business behind it!

The most significant challenge was that brought by Bromley against the GLC, one local authority against another and a key factor was undoubtedly the difference in their political perceptions, one Conservative and the other Labour. A similar political make up can be found in the relationship between Solihull and the West Midlands County Council, the latter several times having been under threat of action by the former. However, a difference of view is definitely not enough as other Conservative councils in London did not rate Bromley's proposed challenge as likely to succeed and rejected an offer of participation as a waste of money. Nevertheless the threat of a challenge may be a sufficient stimulus to change course; the indication by the London Borough of Camden that it disputed the legality of the higher fares introduced following the House of Lords' ruling and was thinking of seeking judicial review contributed to the pressure on the GLC to find a way of reducing fares despite the initial belief of its officers that that was not legally feasible.

Politicans within an authority could also mount a challenge against action proposed by the majority party. This only seemed to occur to the members of one authority in which there was an extremely restrictive attitude to transport support which was arguably in breach of the statutory duty to identify the needs of the community. The idea of a challenge was dropped when it became apparent that there was no support at the party headquarters in view of the improbability of the party gaining majority control.

The Auditor, with his duty to keep a watching brief on the authority and without the burden of costs, will always be a possible challenge to the legality of decisions taken but in the experience of the local authorities interviewed, he has raised only relatively minor issues (possibly major ones were anticipated by the court cases) and has been satisified by them as to their legality. It is probable that the greater or less likelihood there is of a challenge will influence the behaviour of a local authority and there is certainly greater consciousness of this possibility at present. This is a marked contrast to the period before the **GLC case** when a ratepayer's challenge was not envisaged and the legality of the transport policies was not really doubted.

(c) Resort to counsel's opinion

A resounding confirmation that the law is now more significant for local authorities as a result of the **GLC case** has been the increased reliance on counsel's opinions to resolve problems about the legality of proposed courses of action to be taken by councils. This has had a number of effects, notably to diminish the likelihood of successful challenges to local authority decisions and to enable them to make much more extensive use of their existing powers. A further consequence is that where counsel have been used they have been intimately involved in local authority decision-making and this has given rise to reservations about the appropriateness of this development similar to those discussed in relation to the judicial review process.

Resort to counsel's opinion, that is, the seeking of advice on one or more questions of law from barristers has long been a feature of local authority life. Before the **GLC case** it was, however, relatively infrequent and was generally confined to issues which involved technical rather than policy matters, although in the 1970s a number of councils and PTEs had sought advice about the legality of a policy of free public transport. After the **GLC case** there was an undoubted boom in instructions to counsel and these opinions on the implications of that decision for transport policies in other areas were passed, on a confidential basis, amongst many of the authorities that were concerned about the possibility of a challenge. Although the use of counsel reached an unsurpassed peak in 1982, it is evident that the level of use is still much higher than formerly.

Taking counsel's opinion is by no means a reflex action but for many authorities it will readily be sought where a legal problem arises and the possibility of a legal challenge is considered likely. It is of the utmost importance to appreciate, however, that the primary motive for seeking counsel's opinion is likely to be the fear of personal surcharge and in the case of members, disqualification for office[33] in the event of the Auditor successfully challenging the legality of expenditure, or alleging wilful misconduct, pursuant to the policy decisions taken. By seeking and obtaining a favourable opinion from counsel, this possibility can be effectively removed – even if the policy decision is later declared unlawful.[34]

As one officer put it:

> 'They would go for a Queen's Counsel as a form of insurance – as they could say that members took outside advice from the best source – this has been a factor of life for the last four years.'

This attitude is characteristic of most of the authorities interviewed but the level of use is most extensive in the GLC as, more than any other authority, it seems to operate at the very limits of its powers.

Whilst counsel's opinion may well have saved local authorities from challenge in the courts and enabled them to make greater use of their powers, a number of issues arise out of the way that they are used and of the impact that reliance on them has had on the operation of local government. In particular, it is important to consider how counsel are chosen, the way questions are framed and the way unfavourable opinions are dealt with. Also important is the effect that counsel's opinion has on the conduct of local authority business.

For most of the authorities there appeared to be no particular reason for choosing one counsel as opposed to another, except that he may have acted for them in the past or been recommended by another authority. By and large the choice is left to the officers but in at least two instances, which seemed to reflect dissatisfaction with the relationship between counsel and the officers, an element of political selection was apparent. In one authority where a scheme unconnected with transport was being considered and gave rise to legal problems there was pressure to seek advice from counsel known to be sympathetic to the majority party on the council. An officer observed:

> 'The council had the idea that seeking advice from left-wing lawyers would lead to the 'right' advice but in fact they might be even more restrictive and in this case, while the senior was in the Labour Party, it was the junior who was not, who gave the less restrictive advice.'

In another instance frustration at conflicting advice from within the authority (including that of the existing counsel) and advice from outside pressure groups, coupled with allegations by a committee chairperson that the legal

98

officer was out of sympathy with the council's policies, led to a change in counsel, to one noted for his success in representing other councils in conflict with central government.

However, probably more important than the choice of counsel is the way in which the question put is framed. Certainly the fact that counsel is not in sympathy with the political ambitions of the authority does not mean he will not be able to advise them in a way which can secure their fulfilment. Indeed, one counsel responsible for advising the GLC on a wide range of matters, including transport, had written to his own London borough arguing for a challenge to the legality of the supplementary precept! In fact he saw political differences as an advantage in giving advice:

'It helps to differ politically ... one can see the other side.'

The question asked, on the other hand, will in many ways determine the answer given. As one member put it:

'the question put is very important - if it is how far can I go the answer will be broader than if the question is have I gone too far or what can I do.'

The importance of this distinction was also confirmed by the counsel interviewed as the former enabled him to explain the steps needed to be taken to achieve a particular end and this course was followed in relation to the groundwork for the Direction to the LTE at the end of 1982. However, the importance of question setting can have a negative as well as a positive effect and in one authority it was certainly the main theme the contact between officers and counsel had effectively tied the hands of the authority with regard to its transport subsidy.

When advice is sought the councils will naturally hope for favourable advice but in some instances where this has not been obtained they have looked for other advice rather than give up the fight. In such authorities it is clear that the members are not intimidated by the process and it is just seen as one of the many weapons to be used in the defence of their policies. However, members in some of the councils interviewed seemed to have a godlike awe of counsel which approached fear and this, together with the ritual of a special trip to London and a special sense of urgency arising out of an attack on their policy, meant that they did not demur when the advice given in response to a question framed by a member was negative to their policy.

Such cases illustrated how easily counsel's opinion can supplant the decision-making powers of an elected body unless there are members with the confidence and political

99

will to resist. But, even if the members are not craven
and counsel is seen as only there to assist, there is no
doubt that his advice can still have a significant impact
on decision-making. As we indicated when discussing the
role of counsel in advising on fiduciary duty, there is, as
a result, a grave danger of the role of the elected body
being undermined. As one officer put it:

> 'The problem is that people take decisions on the basis
> of what counsel say the courts are likely to do. You
> go to counsel as a practical necessity, in case you are
> challenged. It doesn't make for better decisions, it
> just diffuses the responsibility for those decisions
> ... Its a nice end - stop. But it is a job the
> Council should be doing.'

There is also evidence that counsel's opinion, as well as
that of the Auditor, on questions relating to the legality
of expenditure, has been sought in order to influence
decision-making and further the policy aims and objectives
of both members and politically motivated officers. The
use of legal opinions as a resource in the political
battles which occur within town halls, may be of
considerable significance in terms of the role which law
and lawyers then begin to play in the day-to-day decision-
making processes of local government. It is also
interesting to note that such evidence for this as exists,
suggests that the opinions are not used in party political
clashes, but are relied upon by a faction within the
political grouping which has control in order to emerge
victorious in a struggle over policy. Alternatively, the
opinion forms the basis of a clash between controlling
group members and senior officers in which it is not
always, or only, the latter who are relying on counsel's
opinion, or advice from the Auditor. Clashes of this kind
can be damaging to the officer/member relationship, with
the added complication that chief solicitors or the like
have traditionally seen it as being their perogative to
decide whether counsel's opinion should be sought and from
whom it should be obtained. Some have, therefore, resented
being told both to obtain an opinion, and to go to a
particular QC. They may also have had to contend with
being bypassed by members seeking advice independently
through, for example, the services of trade unions who will
be affected by the outcome of the policy debate. Moreover,
some local authority Solicitors have felt at the very
least, uneasy, about seeking second and third opinions when
the initial advice has been unfavourable. Such
developments represent a politicisation of law and legal
processes which is difficult for some to come to terms
with. But, if these developments have created difficulties
or raised issues relating to the role of lawyers within
local government, they have also highlighted important
questions for the legal system and the role of counsel's
opinion. Politicisation of functions has not stopped at
the door of the town hall lawyer. It is now firmly in
place in the chambers of senior counsel.

Notes

1. A reformulation of these categories has recently been put forward by Lord Diplock in **Council of Civil Service Unions v. Minister for the Civil Service** [1985] A.C. 3774, at p.410, where he identified three heads: illegality, procedural impropriety and irrationality. Whether this formulation will supercede earlier ones remains to be seen.

2. See, e.g., J. Dignan, 'Policy Making, Local Authorities and the Courts'; The 'GLC Fares' Case', (1983) 99 **L.Q.R.** 605; O. Lomas, 'Law as a Resource', in S. Ranson, G. W. Jones and K. Walsh, **Between Centre and Locality: The Politics of Public Policy,** Allen & Unwin, 1985, pp.81-99; O. Lomas, 'Local Government, The Courts and the Law - A Growing Acquaintance', **Local Government Studies,** 1982, vol.9 no.4, pp.23-38; J. A. G. Griffith, 'Judicial Decision Making in Public Law', [1985] Public Law 564, at p.578 **et seq.** More generally, see P. Craig, **Administrative Law,** Sweet & Maxwell, 1983, pp. 366-368; C. Harlow and R. Rawlings, **Law and Administration,** Weidenfeld & Nicholson, 1984, pp.337-339; and M. Loughlin, **Local Government, The Law and the Constitution,** Local Government Legal Society Trust, 1983, chs. 3 & 7.

3. With the exception of Lord Diplock who took a different view.

4. According to Lord Scarman; [1982] 1 All E.R. 129 at p.175.

5. [1955] Ch. 210.

6. In this case, a scheme to provide free travel to old age pensioners had been declared unlawful on the basis that it was implicit in the legislation confirmed that 'ordinary business principles' were to be used in setting fares.

7. See section 7(6).

8. [1982] 1 All E.R. 129, at p. 162.

9. See further, Loughlin, **op. cit.,** p. 42.

10. In the talk referred to in chapter two at note 1.

11. Section 13(3) notices related to the amount of subsidy to be given by the Metropolitan County to the PTE.

12. **R. v. Merseyside** C.C., **ex p. Great Universal Stores Ltd.,** (1982) 80 L.G.R. 639.

13. **R. v. London Transport Executive, ex p. GLC** [1982] 2 All E.R. 262.

14. The emergence of the Divisional Court as a de facto specialist 'Administrative Court' (on which see L. Blom-Cooper, 'The new face of judicial review', [1982] **Public Law** 250 and 353) is seen as likely to result in it taking a different view of administrative action to that of the higher courts; see, e.g., Loughlin, **op. cit.**, at pp.118-9 and 121-2.

15. The Transport Act 1978 s.1(5) gave them power to 'make grants towards any costs incurred by persons carrying on public passenger transport undertakings'.

16. See the famous words of Lord Russell in **Kruse v. Johnson** [1982] 2 Q.B. 91, at p.100. See also D. G. T. Williams, 'The Control of Local Authorities', in J. A. Andrews (ed.), **Welsh Studies in Public Law**, Cardiff, 1970, p.125.

17. See, e.g., **Secretary of State for Education and Science v. Tameside Metropolitan Borough Council** [1977] A.C. 1014, particularly Lord Wilberforce at p.1051.

18. [1983] 1 All E.R. 602.

19. **Ibid**, p.628.

20. They are themselves part of a wider issue; the court was engaged in an effort to limit the review of discretion to the 'improper purpose' or 'total unreasonableness' grounds - of which regard to irrelevant considerations or failure to have regard to all relevant considerations would merely be **evidence**. The judgment of Mr Justice Forbes also includes a clear and strong statement that the weight given to relevant considerations (even if that be nil, provided that it **has been considered**) is not a matter for the courts; see p.621. For further discussion see C. Crawford, 'Auditor, Local Government and the Fiduciary Duty', [1983] **Public Law** 248.

21. [1948] 1 K.B. 223.

22. See, e.g., Loughlin, **op. cit.**, ch.7.3; Dignan, **op. cit.**, p.639 **et seq.**; Lomas, **op. cit.**, (1985), pp.91-94 and (1982) pp.24-25; J. Griffiths, 'Fares Fair or Fiduciary Foul', (1982) 41 **C.L.J.** 216; Crawford, **op. cit.**, pp.252-4 and P. Craig, **op. cit.**, pp.366-8.

23. See R. Buxton, **Local Government** (2nd ed.), Harmondsworth, 1973, pp. 112-6 and Williams, **op. cit.**, pp.132-3.

24. [1955] Ch.201, 235.

25. Lord Diplock saw the existence of the duty as 'throwing light' on the construction of the statute; [1982] 1 All E.R. 129, at p.166.

26. [1925] A.C. 578.

27. This is clear despite the fact that Lord Diplock judged the GLC's decision to be extremely thriftless and could, therefore, have condemned it as an example of 'total unreasonableness' under the **Wednesbury** principles.

28. See note 8 above.

29. See Loughlin **op. cit.**, pp.115-7.

30. **Ibid.**

31. Griffiths, **op. cit.**; Dignan, **op. cit.**, and Lomas **op. cit.**

32. But see Griffith, **op. cit.**, p.575 **et seq.**

33. Under sections 19 and 20 of the Local Government Finance Act 1982.

34. Section 19(3) provides a defence for unlawful expenditure if, **inter alia**, it was believed that the expenditure was 'authorised by law'.

7 On local government

The series of legal challenges to and judgments on the
public transport policies of the GLC and a number of the
Metropolitan County Councils (hereafter collectively
referred to as Metropolitan Authorities) has undoubtedly
had a considerable impact upon the working of those
councils as well as upon councils not directly involved in
judicial process. The organisation and process of
decision-making, as well as the nature of authority and
accountability, have all been influenced by the new climate
of litigation in local government. This impact upon the
activities of local authorities has been reinforced by the
uncertainty which has arisen directly from the perceived
threat of litigation and doubt surrounding its outcome.
The 'threat of litigation is ubiquitous' commented an
official of the GLC, while a member of a Metropolitan
County said:

> 'we keep thinking we are going to be challenged ... it
> makes for great uncertainty.'

We shall propose that the effect of judicialisation and
its incipient uncertainty upon the working of local
authorities has been to make decision-making more:

- formal and procedural
- visible and public

We shall consider each in turn before discussing the
implications of these developments for the accountability
of local goverment.

1. Formality and procedures in decision-making

The changing legal context of the Metropolitan
Authorities has generated a pre-occupation with
demonstrating reasonableness of action. This has
reinforced a concern for procedure and routine in decision-
making as well as a more formalised analysis of relevant
and irrelevant factors. One Head of Transport was
particularly explicit about this new trend:

'one lesson of the case was the importance of procedure
in decision-making ... process is very important. We
were moving from an era of panic to a concern with
procedures - a new ritual - all questions to be asked,
all disadvantages, interests of ratepayers to be borne
in mind before any recommendation could be reached ...
Judges were now concerned not only with merits but also
procedure'.

'The members were advised that if one goes through the
appropriate procedures one could move away from the
business approach - drawing up transport plans,
consulting and assessing needs would allow one to
strike balance between business needs and meeting the
needs of the metropolitan area.'

The routine compliance with procedure reveals adherence
to considered phases and balancing of interests in
decision-making. But at the heart of the growth of
procedure is the felt need for rigorous analysis and
preparation of policy papers and reports to show the
fairness and legitimacy of the decision. Procedure is
integral to the justifying of decisions. Thus an
authority's Solicitor:

'I have already stated that there is a larger degree
of, a larger number of, matters in respect of which
legal advice is put to Committee. In putting legal
advice to the Committee great care is taken in the
preparation of reports: we're concerned to see that
all relevant factors are in the report and no
irrelevant factors to ensure that the decision will
meet with the test of reasonableness. There is a far
greater consciousness of the need for reports to be
properly set out. The justification of decisions is
recognised as being more important.'

A Chairman of Transportation in one of the Metropolitan
Counties underlined the significance of showing analysis as
part of the routine process of justifying decisions. This
authority had been advised that it must show a balance
between capital and revenue expenditure and to show that
all relevant factors of policy had been taken into account
in formulating budgetary decisions. To this end senior
officers adopted a sophisticated cost-benefit analysis

which demonstrated £3 of benefit for each £1 spent and thus the reasonableness of the authority's fares subsidies policies.

The need to demonstrate the reasonableness of the policy process by routinely consulting political and legal interests has led to greater formality in the organisational arrangements of decision-making - in short, to greater bureaucracy.[1] Accompanying the increase in rules and procedures are an extension in the amount of time spent in formal meetings and a growth in paperwork. In some authorities there has been an increase in the specialisation of roles and tasks.

The 'decision-making process is more bureaucratic now', reported one PTE Director: 'our work has become more formalised and there are more meetings'. A Chief Executive re-inforced the notion of growing formalisation in the work of the authority as a result of legislation:

'we generate a lot more paper ...

There is a ritualistic putting down of factors. There is more, longer, writing down of relevant factors and irrelevant factors in decisions. We are now setting down many things that were previously implicitly understood.'

The bureaucratising of the authority's decision-making in the view of this Chief Executive had contributed to increased efficiency in the running of the organisation:

'time, paperwork, following procedures ritualistically for its own sake; the lack of acceptance of experience and tacit understanding, all contrive to lengthen and complicate the decision process.'

A senior solicitor in one authority believed that delay and inaction were caused by the need to meet continually to unravel the grey areas of discretion and the existence of powers to act.

In order to gain reassurance about the legality of their actions local authorities are now routinely seeking the advice of counsel. As one concerned Chief Executive put it:

'if this case isn't a just once in ten years process and is well based in law and precedent, then administrative law becomes another tier of executive government.'

The taking of legal advice, of visiting counsel, has now become an established feature of these local authority's policy making process. The perceptions of the Chief

Executive are supported by those of a Solicitor and a
Director of Transport:

'Every facet of the work was carried out in
consultation and with advice from counsel ... The
House of Lords decision had this effect not only [in
our Authority] but generally in local government. It
was recognised that far more of the decision-making
process required to have legal advice than in the past.
A large number of reports to Committee are now
accompanied with a concurrent report from the legal
department and the most important cases ... are subject
to counsel's advice.'

The Director of Transport reported that they 'now seek
advice on an extensive scale - a fresh mind looking at the
problem can see how a court might interpret the words of an
Act'.

Yet one PTE Director while conceding the growth in
bureaucracy in his organisation as a result of litigation
and the judicial process, nevertheless argued that there
had been beneficial consequences. The growing burden of
rules, meetings and paperwork has constrained the PTE to
clarify roles, as well as the hierarchy of authority and
decision-taking:

'The system is more bureaucratic now. But we also
delegate more. We have analysed all that we do and
found that we are dealing with detail at an executive
level. These changes have been caused both by the
legal and political context. The Executive must
clarify policies, strategies, legality of decisions,
its relationship to the County Council and to
Government. If we are to do all this we must shed
detail ...

Our work has become more formalised. There are more
meetings. But there is more delegation - and we have
been made more accountable. It has accelerated things
which we should have done of our own accord.'

Constrained by legal and political pressure an authority
has been encouraged to clarify its organisation of
authority and decision-making. The growth of bureaucracy
in this instance at least had initiated a more effective
organising of policy and delivery of service.

Whether bureaucratisation has led to inefficiency or not,
the intention and direction of the changes remains the same
- to introduce greater clarity and visibility into the
organisation. Procedures ritually ensure that factors and
interests are taken into account, meetings formally bring
together interests whose statements and agreements are
clearly minuted, while roles and authority become more

clearly defined. Bureaucracy is a device to make explicit
and public that which may previously have been implicit and
private.

2. Visible and public decision-making

Formality and procedures are designed to ensure legality
in decision-making and also a more visible, public,
decision process. Being reasonable is no longer enough.
The Metropolitan Authorities have to be seen to be
reasonable, to demonstrate publicly that their policies
have been arrived at in a reasonable manner. This requires
both greater explicitness - making clear how and why the
decision has been arrived at and visibility - that the
decision process is open to public view.

A senior officer articulated the new explicitness:

> 'a lot of things we did were implicit. You didn't have
> to repeat every six months all the factors surrounding
> a budget - not go through the primer every time. Now
> we have to be **seen** to go through due process. We have
> to set it all down. That's probably desirable but only
> marginally so.'

The idea that judicialisation was constraining the
Metropolitan Authorities to make their decision-making more
public and visible was emphasised by the leader and
Chairman of Transportation in one of the Metropolitan
Counties. The Chairman argued that they were now exhorted
to ensure that policies were formed in the public arena of
the council chamber rather than in private caucases:

> 'in the past we had decided our policies in group, in
> the caucus, and we had not debated them in council:
> therefore, it was argued we had failed to discharge our
> public duty and we would be liable to be surcharged ...
>
> So we had to be seen to be constructing our policies
> of the party in the Council Chamber. We were told that
> the group had to form its policies in public. It was
> not good enough to form policies in private and then
> debate in Council.'

The Solicitor of the authority supported this
interpretation of events following the court proceedings
against it: 'decision-making has been brought back into
the Council arena'.

The Chairman of Transportation suggested that it was
often very difficult to construct a debate in open forum
and to try and get the opposition to respond constructively
so that policy could be seen to emerge from the debate in
council chamber. The opposition would often resist being
drawn into playing their assigned role in the new game.

The more elaborate process of public debate also contributes, the Chairman believed, to delay in decision-making:

> 'on the budget for example, I never shut anybody up for fear of curtailing public debate.'

Decision-making in the Metropolitan Authorities became more explicit and public in the wake of judicialisation.

The injunction that councils should be seen to be taking decisions reasonably and thereby taking into account all relevant factors, has also led them to engage in wider processes of consultation with interested parties:

> 'politicians and bureaucrats now spend a lot more time out and about meeting with pressure groups, unions etc. The whole process has become more complex.'

Councils seek to demonstrate reasonableness and balance in decision-making by ensuring that as wide a range of political interests have been taken into account. Can it be said however that the effects of judicialisation upon local authority decision-making has made them more accountable?

3. Legality and accountability

The pressures upon local authorities to demonstrate the legality of their decision-making may, some believe, have diminished their accountability. Because accountability implies clarity of authority and responsibility so that individual persons, committees or councils can be clearly held to account for decisions taken, the process of judicialisation can be said to have weakened accountability by diffusing responsibility and thus eroding authority. Others, however, claim that the influence of the recent court cases has been to increase accountability and to extend local authorities responsible discretion. Further discussion of these competing claims can be clarified by elaborating the concept of accountability.

The many layers of meaning need to be unravelled if sense if to be made of the emerging institutional forms of accountability. To be accountable is 'to be held to account' but also 'to give an account'.[2] These elements reveal the distinctive social characteristics bound up in the accountable relationship: relations of control but also of discourse. **Being held to account**, therefore defines rather formal ties of control between the parties in an accountable relationship[3], one of whom is answerable to the other for the quality of their actions and performance:

> '... accountability ... involves being called upon to give an account, sometimes mandatorily, but always with a clear and special responsibility.'[4]

This answerability may be for the effective use of public resources or for the delivery of competent professional skills and services. There is, as Stewart[5], calls it, 'a bond' in the accountable relationship: to say that somebody is accountable to assert that there is a duty to account, that he or she is obliged to do so.

To be held to account, however, also provides an opportunity to give an account, to offer a narrative which interprets and explains what has been happening. Those who are held to account are invited to elaborate the purposes and the values which inform their activities:

'The idea of accountability in everyday English gives cogent expression to the intersection of interpretive schemes and norms. To be accountable for one's activities is both to explicate the reasons for them and to supply the normative grounds whereby they may be justified.'[6]

Purpose as well as power are brought together in the institutional arrangements of accountability.

This conceptual understanding of accountability can help us clarify the implications of judicialisation for accountable decision-making in local government. The court cases have, in many ways, had the desirable effect of making local authorities **more** accountable. They have been held to account - either in the courts or in public committees - and their conduct has been subject to closer public scrutiny than before. Local authorities now believe they have to be more explicit in their decision-making giving more formal consideration to all the relevant considerations. This is a beneficial development in public accountability.

Although officers and members would not resist and would welcome an increase in public accountability our study suggests that some of the effects of judicialisation have in practice been detrimental to accountability either because the responsibilities for decision-taking have become confused or because the growth of paperwork necessary to justify decisions can in practice prevent members digesting all the material upon which they need to take decisions.

One Chief Executive expressed particular concern about the impact of judicialisation upon the accountability of members:

'the effect of the court case has been detrimental to the accountability of elected members. Even before the case they used not to read all their papers - now its impossible for them as there are too many. But they can't tell us to cut them down; they can't take the

110

gamble, because they need the protection in case a decision is challenged.'

This view was confirmed by a member in another Metropolitan County. A mountain of papers were presented to the members of the Transportation Committee only hours before the meeting was due to take place and as such made it impossible for the members to digest the material and thus contribute sensibly to debate. The procedures and paperwork now required by law to demonstrate the reasonableness of the decision-process has had the unintended consequence of distancing members from the decisions taken.

The Metropolitan Authorities were also concerned about more serious implications of judicialisation for the accountability of members. The inclusion of counsel's advice and perhaps judicial interpretation on a routine basis has helped only to confuse responsibility for decisions taken:

'the problem is that people take decisions on the basis of what counsel say the courts are likely to do. You go to counsel as a practical necessity, in case you are challenged. It doesn't make for better decisions, it just diffuses responsibility for those decisions.'

This formalising of legal advice leads, as we have noted earlier, to Administrative Law becoming:

'another tier of executive government, either explicitly or implicitly by counsel's interpretation of what he thinks the judges will decide on certain issues.'

The intrusion of the legal soothsayers erodes the authority of elected members in quite a fundamental way because it introduces a new form of decision-making into local government. In place of decision-making by lawfully elected representatives whose judgments are based upon common sense experience is substituted a new technical form of decision-making by experts whose judgments are based upon specialist knowledge of the law:

'the problem comes when the decision-making processes of local government are held up against the decision-making processes of judicial review and of the audit. Decision-making in local government is carried out by officers bringing before members matters requiring decision - it is members who are lay people who have to take the decisions. They don't have the ability/capacity to spend five days on an issue and examine in the same detail as occurs in judicial review - arguing over the meaning of a word, different views on a particular aspect etc.'

The political and professional decision processes of local government are necessarily different in kind.

Some of our respondents, especially senior members, believe that this institution of a more technical expert form of decision-making undermines the democratic accountability of the institution of local government as a whole. A Chief Executive believed that the continual taking of legal advice produced inertia:

> 'I have the greatest respect for counsel, but its at a price in time. The whole process stops us doing other things we should be doing - it diminishes our capacity to do the job.'

The leader of one of the Metropolitan Counties elaborated upon that 'job' as the very process of local government:

> 'For generations in local government we understood that if you put something in your manifesto and you got elected you got on and did it. This was the myth we carried with us for generations.'

He believed the effect of the court cases would erode the very process of local democracy: of parties defining a programme of action, presenting it to the public through public manifesto and submitting it to election and if elected being held to account in a future election according to their performance in government. This leader believed that the process of electoral representation had been frustrated by the law although the Party had been scrupulously open and honest with the public. A deep sense of futility had replaced the initial enthusiasm of election. Who would want to bother with the struggle to gain election to local authorities in future, was his concluding conjecture:

> 'the result is self-evident. The vigour that once existed will quite naturally be dissipated. That members will become time-servers rather than active servers of the public trying to make life better for them. That our towns and cities will become more drab and the type of person you will get who wants to come into local government will be stereo-typed do-gooders rather than those who are genuine representatives of the people.'

The capacity for local government to act and to be held to acount for their actions has been considerably diminished.

Local authorities, therefore, are increasingly held to account. The way that this works out in practice can be a constraint upon accountability. And yet being held to account provides an opportunity for local authorities to present 'an account' of their purposes and the reasons for their actions. The process of judicialisation - becoming more akin to court processes - implies increasing dialogue and discourse: opinions are examined by a process of dialectic in which parties are challenged to give an account that provides reasons or grounds for the claims put forward[7] has emphasised that much can depend upon skill and performance in presenting an account. The dramaturgical images of the theatre are aposite in the accounting of a script from actor to audience.

Many local authorities have grown to realise the opportunities for them in the accounting process as a result of judicialisation. Because the court cases pointed to uncertainties and differences of perception and interpretation of the law, local authorities have responded by paying more attention to interpretive analysis within their own accounting performance: developing an account which presents their case with great skill and power. The law is now perceived not as a fixed, objective, system of rules but as uncertain, alterable and dependent upon interpretation: upon winning the dialectic. A skilled performance in accounting can ensure victory for a local authority and thus an extension of its powers. Local authorities have become more adept at manipulating the law.

Local authorities are less in awe of the law. They take second opinions, they choose different counsel to suit their desired account. They are not willing to take the law lying down and seek to extend the limits of their powers. One Chief Executive believed that the increased legal climate had extended the limits of the politically possible because local authorities are now continually checking out with lawyers and counsel the limits of their discretion. A senior solicitor reinforced the point:

'It has led us to break new ground in terms of the limits of discretion ... Before when you were faced with something that seemed on the face of it to be unreasonable, you didn't tend to take it further. That was before we were in the position of almost ritualistically putting down all the factors. Now if you go to one of the leading politicians, they can do it almost automatically. There are a number of examples of things we have done that we might not have down before:

- the reception of unemployment marchers

- our publicity campaign

- grants to voluntary bodies

all would have been on the borderline. Similarly with the introduction of equal opportunity measures and various pioneering and campaigning work ... We do test the edges of what we can more.'

The boundaries of political action can be extended and thus the capacity of elected representatives to deliver policies to their electorate enhanced and made more secure. Judicialisation, therefore, has been educational with local authorities becoming more aware of the fallibility, the political nature of the law. The 'spirit' of an objective law above politics has been broken both by central government's intervention in local government law and by the reluctance of local authorities to accept legal advice without question. This has also been noted by Lord Justice Woolf, when in the Street Memorial Lecture, he said:

> 'It used to be the case that if the legality of a course of action was in doubt, it was not adopted. Now it appears to be coming a case of anything is permissible unless and until it is stopped by the courts.'[8]

The law is now much more centre stage, perceived as a tool in the policy making process. Now, aware of the resourcefulness of the law, local authorities are testing the boundaries of the law.

This trend may be detrimental both for the law as well as for local government. The authority of both has depended upon an unquestioning belief in the political neutrality of the law. Now, the limits of political discretion are given by and **negotiated** with the custodians of the law. The limits of the polity are no more or less than the limits of legal judgment.

Notes

1. cf. M. Weber, 'Bureaucracy', in H. H. Gerth and C. Wright Mills, **From Max Weber: Essays in Sociology,** Routledge and Kegan Paul, London, 1948; P. Blau, **The Dynamics of Bureaucracy,** University of Chicago Press, London, 1955; M. Albrow, **Bureaucracy,** Macmillan, 1970.

2. cf. H. T. Sockett, 'Accountability the Contemporacy Issues' in H. T. Sockett (ed.) **Accountability in the English School System,** Hodder and Stoughton, London, 1980; J. D. Stewart, 'The role of information in Public Accountability', in C. Tomkins (ed.) **Current Issues in Public Sector Accountability,** Phillip Allan, London, 1984; S. Ranson, 'Towards a Political Theory of Public Accountability in Education', **Local Government Studies,** Vol. 12, No. 4, July/August 1986.

3. G. W. Jones, **Responsibility in Government,** London School of Economics, 1977.

4. J. Lello, **Accountability,** Ward Lock, London, 1979.

5. Stewart, **op. cit.**

6. A. Giddens, **The Constitution of Society,** Polity London, 1984.

7. R. Beiner, 'Rescuing the rationalist heritage', **Times Higher Educational Supplement,** June 22, 1984; A. Gray, 'Codes of Accountability and the presentation of an account: Towards a micro-administrative theory of public accountability', **Public Administration Bulletin,** No. 46, December 1984; A. Gray and W. I. Jenkins, **Administrative Politics in British Government,** Wheatsheaf, Thetford, 1985.

8. Sir Harry Woolf, 'Public Law - Public Law: Why The Divide? A Personal View', [1986] **Public Law** 220, 221-2.

PART IV
TOWARDS AN
EXPLANATORY MODEL

8 Towards an explanatory model

The focus of this research has been upon the impact of recent judicial decisions upon the internal relations and decision-making of local authorities in the field of public transportation. The discussion so far has **described** the effect of the court cases in London and the Metropolitan and non-Metropolitan Counties and has **analysed** the effect of increased judicialisation upon the legal and decision-making processes of the local authorities concerned. The analysis has sought to identify and elaborate some of the general patterns of response across the local authorities as well as the differences which exist between them.

At this stage we need to develop our analysis conceptually so as to identify the significant dimensions in the response which local authorities have made to recent judicial decisions. This will enable us to form a typology of responses. The analysis then proceeds theoretically to develop an explanatory framework which seeks to account for the variations between types of response as well as the general patterns of change which is affecting the legal climate of local government. Because at this stage in the analysis we are interested in their response to the court cases as local authorities, we introduce pseudonyms for the Metropolitan Counties in addition to those already used for the non-Metropolitan Counties. The three Metropolitan Counties are referred to as Glebeshire, Loamshire and Marlshire.

1. A typology of responses to judicialisation

Local authorities, we argue, have varied in their response to judicial activism in the field of public transportation along two central dimensions:

. an administrative response

. a political response

   The discussion of the case study authorities and the
subsequent analyses suggest a direct relationship between
the experience of legal challenge, or proximity to
challenge, and the development of more formalised
administrative and decision-making processes within the
local authorities affected. Judicialisation in short,
promotes and sometimes requires, bureaucratisation. In
order to demonstrate the legality of their policies and
programmes - as legal convention now suggests they must in
order to comply with the law - local authorities have been
constrained to introduce much greater formality into their
administrative processes. The reasons for decisions and
policies must be supported by reports and paperwork which
set out in detail the relevant factors; due procedure must
be seen to have been followed; interested parties must be
routinely consulted. A more formalised and standardised
administrative process has not been the only aspect of
bureaucracy to develop. The decision-making process has
become more centralised as strategic decisions about the
taking of legal advice or of the forming of policy have
become concentrated around senior members and officers in
the local authority. A more legalised climate therefore
has forced local authorities to clarify their
organisational structures and processes. Bureaucracy is a
device in this instance as in others to ensure compliance
with procedure and control of decision-making.

   The second significant dimension relates to the political
response which local authorities have made to judicial
challenge and legislation. How compliant have they been in
the face of the use of the law, as they perceive it, to
restrict their manifesto policies of support for public
transportation (as well as other services).
Whereas none of the Metropolitan Authorities we have
studied chose to defy the law, most of them have, by
adaptation, the development of new strategies, and by
operating to the limits of their statutory powers, managed
to adhere to, or even further developmt the broad thrust of
their manifesto commitments. One Metropolitan Authority
however, although not denouncing its manifesto commitments,
has adopted a passive and submissive attitude in the face
of the apparent implications of the fares cases both for
public transport and other new and controversial policies
outlined in its programme. Thus, it has treated judgments
objectively as amounting to a fait accompli and has
retreated from a position of actively seeking to pursue
policies. A typology of the responses of the authorities
to judicialisation is set out in Figure 1.

Figure 1
A Typology of Responses to Judicialisation

	Political Response	
	Submission	Strategic Adaptation
Status Quo	(Rurshire [1])	Urbshire
Administrative Response		
	Bureau- cratisation	Loamshire	London Glebeshire Marlshire

2. Developing an explanatory framework

The analytical task is to develop an explanatory framework that will account for the varying responses of the local authorities in our sample to judicial challenge and judicialisation. Why is it that certain types of response have developed?

The explanatory framework developed here is designed to incorporate elements of both an 'action' perspective with its emphasis on actors striving for power in order to facilitate their interests, and a 'structuralist' perspective with its stress on institutional and environmental constraints which limit the operations of power [2]. Only in this way will it be possible to avoid over simplification of the complexities of local authority decision-making. Seen in this light, the law and judicial decisions may be seen both as a constraint on local authority decisions and, according to interpretation, as a 'resource' to be utilised by various actors in the competition for power and influence over such decisions [3].

Our analysis begins with the assumption that the interpretive procedures of actors within local authorites are central to understanding their policies and their response to recent judicial decisions. The values and beliefs of senior members and officers will shape not only their attitude towards the development of public services such as transportation but also their perceptions and understandings of the law in general and of doctrines such as 'fiduciary duty'. Of course, this type of analysis of internal actors' perceptions of the law has to be sensitively related to changing interpretations within the legal community generally of the importance, for example, of the concept of 'reasonableness' as evidenced by recent developments in case law. More broadly, we argue that underlying and shaping actors' perceptions and interpretations of the law and of the legal effect of judicial decisions are sets of beliefs, values and ideologies they hold about the law itself, about the management of local authorities and about the purpose, status and accountability of public services within democratically elected local government. Those officers and councillors who value the corporate responsibility of their local authorities for the overall cultural, economic and social well-being of their communities may respond to judicial decisions in a different way from those committed to the provision of separate services in order to comply with statutory obligations; those actors ideologically committed to public services may seek different interpretations of the law from those whose belief systems commend managerialism and administrative efficiency. We see the work of McAuslan [4] on the role of ideology and attitudes regarding property, public services and participation in influencing interpretations and the operation of planning law to be generally instructive in this regard. Also we need to relate ideological differences to party and factional divisions among councillors and to variations in professional backgrounds among officers, as well as to their past experiences and positions held within the hierarchy of local authority organisation and decision-making.

This latter factor points to the analytical importance of the concept of power. Not only will the extent to which different values and beliefs influence decision-making vary according to the actors relative positions of power and domination within local authorities, but the effect of increased judicial activity may be to alter power relations within local authorities in favour of certain actors. Thus, beyond any specific policy changes that may have resulted from particular judicial decisions on public transport, they may have led to the introduction of new procedures which, following on from Galanter [5] will themselves bring certain values and considerations to the fore and possibly strengthen the position within the decision-making process of those actors with access to counsel or other sources of legal advice such as auditors, with knowledge about the courts and law and with skill to interpret legal judgments. It would also be important to explore the 'hidden' aspects of power: but also the capacity to define the key issues, to shape agenda and institutionalise legal understandings and values as 'the way things are done here'.

Yet the operation of power and the potential discretion of actors will themselves be constrained by existing institutional arrangements and environmental conditions impinging on local authorities. To make sense of the interpretive procedures and transactions of actors in relation to legislation we need to locate them within a broader context of economic and political restructuring.

3. The framework applied

The explanatory framework set out above can be particularly helpful in accounting for the variations between our case study authorities in their response to legislation. We propose to focus upon the position of Loamshire in relation to the other Metropolitan Authorities, because this requires particular comparative analysis and explanation. It is useful, first, however, to say something further about the case of Rurshire.

(a) Rurshire : political commitment and administrative
      stability

The dimensions informing the typology suggest that judicialisation will have a direct impact on decision-making and organisational arrangements of an authority, while the political response will vary with the pattern of belief and power in each authority.

In many ways a straightforward analysis of choice and constraint can explain what we encountered in Rurshire. Rurshire like Urbshire has not experienced any extension of bureaucratisation as a result of a more legalised climate because they have had no experience of judicial challenge in the field of transportation. Although the authority concurs with the interpretation that judicial activity has increased in recent years - and can cite its own experience to do with school closures, appeal panel cases on school admissions as well as right of way cases - and would also report some effect of this upon the formality and cautiousness of the authority's administration. Yet these legal challenges, though increasing, have not been experienced on the same scale and intensity as those in the Metropolitan Authorities. The trend towards bureaucratisation is however in the expected direction and if the judicial process continues to increase we would anticipate the usual effects upon the rules and procedures of the authority's decision-making.

The distinctiveness of this authority's position in our typology however lies in its positive commitment not only to controlling the development of public services such as transportation, but more significantly propounding a distinctive ideology of market provision in relation to those services. It is the choices of actors in the authority as much as the relative absence of legal contingencies which explains its behaviour.

It is by exploring the values and interpretive procedures of the authority that we can understand much of its actions: not only in relation to policy, but also the law and the relation of the law to the polity.

The politicial persuasion of the authority encourages allegiance to central government policies of constraint upon the provision of public services and moreover allowing provision to be shaped by the operation of market forces. Bus services, for example, should be provided in relation to demand:

'our strategy is to buy off trouble. We can't from the centre assess local rural needs. We can only respond to expressed demand. Those who express their demand loudest receive the most. If there are two areas of equal need then the loudest should win the service ...

Our policy allows natural supply and demand to meet. It is a market mechanism policy. If demand increases naturally (not artifically stimulated by us) then the supply will increase and the local authority would have to raise more revenue support'.

The determining beliefs here comprise assumptions about the public as forming an aggregate of individual consumers rather than forming in any sense a local community, and assumptions about the role of the local authority as a neutral, passive, responder to demand rather than possessing an active interventionist role in defining and shaping the needs of the environment.

Beliefs about the law as well as policy within the interpretive schema of senior members and officers have been important in shaping the response of the authority to judicialisation. The law and legal advice are perceived as a resource to be drawn upon to support the policies of the local authority. Thus the Solicitor of the authority:

124

'we seek counsel's advice to confirm our view, to gain
support if we are challenged ...'

['Who decides what counsel to take?']

'I do. You decide upon someone you know'.

['Are the counsel chosen according to the result you
want?']

'Yes, any solicitor does that! To support your line,
to fight your case, to save some costs against you at
least. You don't choose somebody who says you are up
the pole'.

The more politicised context which faces local
authorities leads them to use the law to support their
chosen ends:

"I must seek a Conservative chosen counsel. It would
be difficult for me to see a Labour counsel. Though I
would never be pressurised by members to take such a
view: they want an 'independent' view".

But the senior legal adviser to the authority knows the
taken for granted rules of the game. Values and
assumptions in this authority have shaped attitudes towards
the law and about the status of the law in relation to the
polity. The leadership is clear that the law is
subservient to the policy, although the law, in all cases,
must be complied with:

'if there is a legal obligation we fulfil it:
Conservatives never break the law for policy'.

Yet the Leader of the authority believes that the erosion
of local discretion and the accelerating centralisation of
power in Whitehall is 'leading to an abuse of legislative
power'. The primacy of the polity derives from a view that
the law cannot resolve cases to do with the balance of
rights within an area. Such decisions are legitimately
political decisions and local authorities must be granted
the necessary powers to respond efficiently to local
demand.

The values and interpretations have shaped much of the
perceptions and actions of Rurshire. But arguably, so has
the operation of power. Rurshire provides a classic study
of 'non-decision making' [6]. Why was it that an authority,
the legality of whose actions were in doubt in refusing to
assess need, was not challenged through the courts? Power
has been used in discrete ways by the authority to suppress
opposition and thus to further its own interpretations and
policies.

The authority denies that it has acted outside the law. The leader knows that there is a duty to assess need but:

> 'we maintain we do it. We could go further in assessing but we would not. It is done on a political judgment basis'.

The argument is that by responding to articulated demand the authority **is** responding to need:

> 'assessing need directly merely produces need and therefore political embarrassment'.

The Leader, however, is well aware that certain communities are less articulate than others and less likely to press their claim that they need bus services:

> 'the traditional working communities in the village are more philosophical. They do not demand'.

He is also aware that the way they respond to demand is arbitrary:

> 'we do more damage by subsidising some routes. At the end of the day the subsidies are arbitrary because we are responding to specific demands, to the interests of the articulate middle classes in the expanded rural villages'.

His rational solution to this arbitrariness of current policy and practice is to give full rein to the market:

> 'I would let the market take its course; subsidy distorts the pattern of services; let the market determine what is provided'.

Although the authority does not believe it has acted illegally, it has been concerned enough to take legal advice. The Solicitor reported that the authority only usually seek external advice when it is challenged, but in this instance advice had been sought in the absence of challenge to test the legality of their practice of not assessing need. The advice did not deter their practice.

The authority acknowledge that the policy of not assessing needs has been opposed by the local Labour Party:

> 'We are the meanest authority ... and ... we are the subject of complaint. Labour would give the public what they think they need, believing that the rural areas are deprived ...
>
> The Opposition Party bring up the issue of need regularly at the Sub-Committee. But we have held off the assessement of need and not yet been challenged'.

Why has there been no challenge when the Opposition has produced a report which presents a clear analysis of unmet need for rural transport?

Elements of what Saunders calls the 'non-decision making filter' [7] are clearly at work in Rurshire. For some of the actors, the rural poor and often their representatives, the grievances to do with inadequate bus services are not even formulated because there is a **'mobilisation of bias'** at work: the beliefs and values of dominant interests are so embedded in local culture and institutions that the idea of formulating a grievance in terms of demands to the local authority often even fail to cross the minds of those whose interests are denied. If grievances are formulated they are sometimes not pressed because of the futility of **'anticipated reactions'**. One of the senior members of the Opposition Party believed that groups in the community were reluctant to press their interests because they felt that there was no point - there was no hope of them winning:

> 'in the city there would have been an outcry. Here many people in the villages are apathetic, they shrug their shoulders, there is a reluctance to challenge those in authority'.

Yet a challenge of a kind was mounted by the Labour Party on behalf of the rural villages but its failure illustrates the weak power bases of the Opposition. Bereft of resources, and skill in applying those it had, left the Opposition defeated and dependent in exchange relations with authority. The Opposition lacked the organisation and political resources to forge alliances which could provide effective opposition. The Sub-Committee councillors could not persuade the Group to give the issue of rural buses its highest priority; they failed to harness the support of the Consultants who had helped with the 'Alternative Plan' or the Parish Councillors who expressed interest. The Labour Party lacked financial as well as political resources to press its demands through the courts. Appeals to the national Labour Party at Walworth Road proved fruitless although the grounds for judicial proceedings were accepted.

Bereft of resources, unable to apply any sanctions, the opposition was powerless to prevent even the processes of non-decision-making within the authority by dominant interests: that is, decisions that result in 'suppression or thwarting of a latent or manifest challenge to the values or interests of the decision-maker' [8].

(b)   Loamshire : reluctant compliance

The reluctant compliance of Loamshire when compared with the continuing resistance of the other Metropolitan Authorities requires explanation.   While all the Metropolitan Authorities shared a common interpretive scheme - all brought to their manifesto for the 1981 election a distinctive set of radical policies for planning and transportation in their regions - one authority retreated from active commitment to the original programme.   The relative distribution of power resources help us to account for the varying responses of the Metropolitan Authorities in response to judicialisation:

.   political resources of membership and composition

.   political control

.   organisational networks and alliances

.   knowledge and skill in applying the rules of the game.

The 1981 elections saw the return of councils which varied considerably in experience and continuity of service.   Whereas the GLC possessed a ruling group of substantial weight and experience, Loamshire was seriously depleted of experienced members following the election. The Leader of that Council reported:

'we were short on talent and experience.   There was a whole host of new councillors who had very little experience.   Of the 31 in opposition prior to the election a number did not fight and this left a caucus of 15 members who had served 4 years in opposition'.

Lacking politically experienced colleagues and appreciating that Transportation was central to their programme, the Leader was forced for the first year to chair this committee on top of his other duties, while he tutored a younger member to assume responsibility later.

The political composition of the group was also a significant factor.   The number and strength of the Manifesto Group (as we might call them) would be important in determining the strength of commitment following the elections.   Whereas in the GLC the Manifesto Group formed a substantial proportion of the caucus as well as the leadership, in Loamshire they were not in a majority - and those prepared to commit themselves to the manifesto policies 'dwindled to less than ten' as one councillor reported.   Doubtful political commitment together with inexperienced membership do not form a likely basis for serious political assertion, or resistance.

The exercise of political leadership over members and officers within the authority varied markedly between GLC and Loamshire. The relationship of members and officers has been particularly important here, especially the degree of consensus about beliefs and understandings. Whereas in all the other Metropolitan Authorities there has existed a common interpretive understanding of the needs of their area and the appropriateness of policies to meet those needs, in Loamshire, however, many of the senior officers had little sympathy for the manifesto policies. A climate of suspicion and distrust developed:

'there are new attitudes between members and officers. Attitudes of distrust. There was in 1981 and there still is a chasm between us in 1984. This arms length relationship is not good for the management of the local authority'.

Nor for activities presupposing unity, agreement and commitment.

In the absence of agreement between members and officers, and this did not always exist in the GLC, one might expect political control. Thus a senior member observed:

'a new administration to county hall ... relied on officers' advice for all policy implementation. The members made it clear what aims were to be achieved - there was wide publicity within the building. **They acted on advice about implementation but there was clear political direction.** They wanted to achieve matters quickly - they didn't want officers to divert them from their goals - people who are uncomfortable about this should leave and this message got through - though there was no intimidation of anyone to act against the law'. (our emphases)

The capacity of the Metropolitan Authorities to build organisational networks and alliances varied considerably and was a contributory factor in accounting for resistance of retreat in the face of legalisation. Loamshire sought counsel's advice as did all the other Metropolitan Authorities but in struggles of this kind it is important to be able to draw upon sources of advice and understanding, to be provided with alternative knowledge and information. Loamshire was not supported by strong organisational networks that comprised interest groups, trades unions or members of parliament.

In London, however, when members of the GLC were at the point of conceding defeat and retreating they were encouraged and reinforced by an extensive network of mutual support; from research departments, trades unions, other local authorities, knowledgeable experts in the field:

'There was a shell-shocked response. No option but to
cut services and raise fares... He couldn't believe it
was the only way to respond to the Lords - others
outside the building, for example, Transport 2000 [NUR
funded]   sought legal advice about the doubling of
fares, as did   Camden. He was asked by the local
trades council to see Platts Mills and Jeremy Smith [9]
on ways round the Law Lords decision - Camden was
doing the same later on. All were saying use the
Greater London Development Plan (GLDP)...

Then Camden's formal challenge [taking the GLC to
court if there was no reduction in fares] came in and
as a result the officers began to take this seriously.
They changed their lawyers - he wanted a socialist
lawyer. Only after the meeting with Platts Mills and
advice from Transport 2000 were they prepared to use
lawyers to retrieve the situation'.

The network of actors provided GLC not only with accurate
information and timely advice but also strategic
intervention on behalf of the beleaguered authority. The
network provided authoritative knowledge for members which
informed their relations with officers and enabled them to
control officers when necessary.

The GLC members and officers were learning and becoming
skilful in the new rules of the game: of selecting
appropriate counsel and, importantly, of demonstrating
'reasonableness' by supporting their arguments with
procedures, consultations and analyses. They were becoming
knowledgeable and innovative in their use of the law. They
rethought ways of achieving their objectives within the
parameters of the law. They approached the problem in
different ways; they asked their counsel to provide
different solutions. They saw the law as a resource. They
had learned to use the law as an instrument which can be
adapted to purposes when supported by documented reasoned
argument. They rethought their position and strategy.

In particular they learned to ask the key question: which
is not 'is it lawful?' but rather 'how can I achieve such
and such?' Whereas the first question invites a limited
and narrow response from lawyers, the second encourages new
approaches and ways of perceiving issues: it asks for
alternative solutions.

Organisation, knowledge and astuteness in learning and
applying the new legal rules of the game do much to account
for the active resourceful pursuit of manifesto policies in
one authority, while their absence accounts for the passive
compliance in the other.

4. The incompleteness of the action account

The typology presented in Figure 1 was constructed to illustrate the significant differences between the local authorities in our sample in response to judicial challenge and legalisation. The action framework has provided an analysis which examines those differences in terms of the interpretive procedures which the actors bring to bear on a situation and their relative power dependencies. The authorities differed in their resourcefulness with respect to the law. This was manifested in the extent to which they were willing and able to wrestle with the law to secure patterns of interpretation which supported their policies. Yet what the authorities have in common may be as important as the features which separate them and to account for them we will need to draw upon a different form of explanatory analysis.

All the Metropolitan Authorities were elected in 1981 on manifestos which proposed radical change intended to regenerate community and economy in metropolitan conurbations. The encounter which these authorities have had with the law since 1981 has restricted the extent to which all of them have been able to implement these ideas and policies.

Loamshire for example, planned - as well as subsidising bus fares - to:

i)   draw upon Pension Funds to support the investment programmes of the authority's Enterprise Board in order to stimulate local industry

ii) subsidise the travel of YTS trainees under a scheme which would have cost half a million pounds

iii) support a Black Business Scheme under which it would invest in and make funds available to businesses owned by blacks

The essential aim of these radical manifesto programmes was to achieve a significant redistribution of local resources in favour of deprived groups or areas in the community. Legal advice ultimately counselled against the adoption of such schemes as the objectives of the policies would either be inconsistent with the purposes considered relevant by courts and/or lawyers to the exercise of the statutory powers to be used (i and ii) or would involve a conflict with the express statutory prohibition on discriminating favourably or unfavourably by reference to racial criteria (iii). There was undoubtedly some scope for adaptability in the methods that could be used to achieve the overall objectives: thus a Black Business Scheme could have been recast as a scheme to assist businesses in economically run-down areas which would have helped the intended beneficiaries without doing so on a racial basis. Nevertheless, such adaptability was not always an option (regardless of whether it was welcome to the policy-makers) as the experience of the extremely ingenious and skilful GLC demonstrated:

'There have been a number of policy initiatives which they couldn't take following advice e.g. concessionary fares for the unemployed. Sometimes they have been told not to pursue a policy beyond a certain point for example, employment on LT. GLC does not want to destroy jobs but counsel say LT must be efficient, economic and integrated so it can't have jobs for the sake of jobs ... [although] security or passenger assistance could be reasons for increasing jobs'.

The hurdles or barriers which the law put in the way of implementing many social policies came to be seen as incompatible with traditional understandings of the political process of a party placing policies before an electorate which, if supported, it then puts into practice and for which it is held to account in the following election. Thus, the Leader in Loamshire commented:

'For generations in local government we understood that if you put something in your manifesto and you got elected you got on and did it. This was the myth we carried with us for generations'.

The obstacles in the path of any accommodation between the law and radical (socialist) politics can be clarified by an explanatory perspective which makes sense of the common underlying structural patterns as well as the differences and variations between authorities.

5. **The law in its social and political context**

The action framework proposes that, if we lay bare the competing interests and purposes of actors, we have contributed much of the explanation of the circumstances we wish to understand. Another perspective argues that we can only make sense of these intentions and purposes by setting them in context and by theorising the relationship between context and action. This perspective proposes that we examine the structure of social systems (the way parts relate to each other) and to see change as deriving from the dilemma of maintaining the system (or as some argue the infrastructure of the system).

We argue that we can only make sense of the emerging patterns of judicial action and local authority decision-making by seeing them in the context of economic, social and political change. The economic crises of the mid-1970s was generated by the Middle East War, stagnant production levels and spiralling inflation. The recession placed inevitable pressures upon public expenditure and services. Yet, however important these fiscal changes were, they have been overshadowed by structural changes in employment: the shedding of surplus is now beginning to raise fundamental questions about the place of work in people's lives and thus their source of income. Cyclical and structural changes in the economy parallel and reinforce social and political change: social trends show an aging society, more fragmented family patterns, inner city stress, alienation and boredom. The extent of such change is leading to more politicised responses as conceptions of resolving economic and social problems sharpen.

The significance of the 1981 County Council Elections for our subject lies in this context. The elections saw the return of local Labour parties committed to radical programmes of social and economic change. Many of our interviewees located their own interpretation and analysis of judicialisation in the context of these elections:

'Transportation is the wrong starting point for the increased judicialisation of local government. The 1981 election is the turning point'.(Solicitor)

'The background to the case was that the Labour party was elected to a majority hold of the GLC in 1981 on the basis of and strongly committed to a detailed public manifesto which included a policy commitment to a substantial increase in public transport use encouraged by a 25 per cent reduction in fares as a first step .... There was a clear change on the part of the incoming Labour administration. There was a determination to set out their policy and then to stick to it. In a sense that determination was born of a belief on their part that bureaucracy tended to get in the way and therefore there was a marked difference in style'. (Chief Executive)

'1981 was a landmark ....The manifesto commitment by Labour was critical. More weight was attached to that than in any previous Labour administration - every report on services still has to refer to the relevant manifesto commitment'. (Head of Transportation)

'1981 saw the rise of the left wing militants ... The
problem is that the County Council sees itself as an
alternative government with rights over Loamshire. The
left wants a switch of resources to the working class:
that is what is behind the YTS fares subsidy issue'.
(PTE Director)

The 1981 election saw a breaking of the boundaries of
local politics as well as a disturbing of the conventional
relationships between members and officers. The election
of radical parties at local level intensified argument and
disagreement about the appropriateness of policies and the
discretion of local authorities.

The breaking of boundaries at local level, however, was
part of a wider collapse of consensus in the polity
nationally and, in particular, in the relations between
central and local government. Central government's
strategy to contract public expenditure reflected not only
a reaction to the fiscal crisis but altered views about the
status of public services [10]. The post-war consensus
belief in the welfare state as well as a planned economy
suffered a fundamental reversal with the 1979 general
election. The Government's plans to centralise control
over public expenditure and thus local government was the
centre's response both to a transformed economic and social
context but also to developments in local government,
illustrated by the 1981 County Council elections, which saw
the emergence of a radical socialism at local level.

Central government was developing its own steering
capacity of controls and domination to cope with a changed
context. This restructuring of relations between central
and local government had direct implications for the
'reasonableness' of local authorities' policies and thus
the legality of their spending:

  'the basis of my concern on the question of
  reasonableness related to the whole issue of the
  consensus about the comparative positions of central
  and local government. There had been an understanding
  about the extent to which one would respect the other,
  and it was abundantly clear to me that the introduction
  of penalties into the grant system was by its nature,
  scale and arbitrariness a breach of this understanding.
  The whole basis of 'reasonableness' had been busted
  wide open. This was particularly so in the case of
  London and the GLC where the penalty factor was as high
  as four - in most other authorities it was considerably
  less'. (Senior GLC Officer)

The suggestion, therefore, is that reasonableness presupposes agreed understandings about institutional arrangements within the polity and about the programmes which they should pursue.

The state has been reordering institutional arrangements to tighten its control of local government in general and the radical Metropolitan Authorities in particular. The incipient processes of legalisation need to be examined in this changing economic and political context. What consequences did the use of the law have for the workings of the local authorities? How do we interpret its function in this changing context?

The values of radical politics and the values expressed in law and by the judiciary came into direct conflict in the sphere of local government after 1981. The values expressed in radical (socialist) politics sought to redistribute resources and services in favour of the disadvantaged sections of the community: for example the unemployment, the poor, the black and ethnic minorities. These political values are inconsistent with the ideologies of fairness and private (property) rights embodied in law and as interpreted by the judiciary which resist local government conferring benefit on groups of the population at the expense of ratepayers.

We argue that the law operated to control the policies and operations of local authorities by influencing ideologically the way that they were to regard their services. Legal ideologies supportive of private (property) rights and traditional notions of fairness which stipulate equal treatment for all were used to frustrate many political programmes seeking to favour the economically disadvantaged sections of the community. These ideologies or values may manifest themselves in a number of ways. They may be reflected in express statutory provisions such as the Race Relations Act 1976 which contains a very clear prohibition on the use of racial criteria in the award of grants and which was used to stifle proposals for a Black Business Scheme in Loamshire. More often, however, they will emerge or be reinforced by courts and lawyers in the course of their interpretation of the enabling powers conferred by Parliament. Where this happens the decision may in some cases simply confirm the understanding of those using the power. Equally, however, the outcome may result in the surprise seen in the **GLC case**. Once the decision has been taken by a court and is not subject to any further appeal then those values/approaches to interpretation will become the orthodoxy (however unpalatable) and should, at least in formal, doctrinal terms, be as clear as an express statutory prohibition.

This is not, however, always the case as is apparent from the discrepancy between the highly restrictive view as to the possibility of supporting LTE through grants taken by the GLC and its officers and the more flexible approach adopted by central government which was supported in the ruling in the case brought by the GLC against the LTE. [12]

As we have indicated many of the senior officers and members involved in the judicial process during and after the transport cases were extremely surprised that there was such scope for different interpretations to be placed upon statutory provisions:

'The things that disturbed me about the process were... the games that were played at not having regard to Hansard ... It seems to me that it was self-evident, without knowing about public transport, what the structure of the Act meant in its own right ... the Act was hierarchical.

What absolutely reinforced that was to have lived through the period since the war in local government and knowing that the 1969 Act represented a major change in public administration relating to public transport. The Act was so very much different from previous public transport acts. You couldn't help asking why it was so different. I can't now understand how it was possible for the Law Lords to read the Act the way they did ... I was absolutely shattered by the decision in the House of Lords. I still am. I have never got over it and never will. They couldn't possibly have reached that judgment'.

The law is a complex instrument open to manifold interpretations and influences often reflecting the conflicting ideologies which underlie the purposes of public law: whether its role is, for example, to protect private (property) rights, or to facilitate government action in what is perceived to be the collective or the public interest. [12]

The interpretations of the judiciary in the transport cases drew upon particular traditions and understandings of the role of the law. In particular, the Law Lords stressed that the transport undertakings in London should operate on 'ordinary business principles'. This finding was not inevitable. It arose from the court's interpretation of the case of **Prescott v Birmingham Corporation** [13] in 1955 in which a scheme to allow free travel to elderly people had been declared unlawful on the basis that the statute governing the transport undertaking required that fares be fixed 'in accordance with business principles'. If one examines this case it is clear that the court was not laying down a general principle yet the

House of Lords' finding was to elevate this decision to a general principle of the law, the applicability of which was to be presumed unless the relevant statute provided otherwise. This finding was of critical importance. It alone made the outcome of the **GLC case** inevitable, and effectively determined the highly controversial issue of whether public transport should be run on semi-business lines, or as a social service:

> 'It is apparent from the judgment that the primary consideration which led the House of Lords to their decision, was that any departure from 'ordinary business principles' would involve additional subsidies, the cost of which would have to be borne by the ratepayers. By interpreting the statutory provision in the way that they did, and making an 'ordinary business principles' presumption, this could however be avoided and the interests of ratepayers protected. The ideological basis of their decision can, therefore, be seen to be a desire to minimise the amount of private financial resources which could be legitimately appropriated to contribute to the cost of providing public transport, and, therefore, the redistributive dimension of the statutory provisions. Ultimately, therefore, their decision was based upon the ideology of private property'. [14]

There is, however, nothing new in the values adhered to by judges determining the interpretations given to legislation. It is part and parcel of the natural choices involved in law making. The judicial element may run with the parliamentary input or may run counter to it; in the latter case this is where the courts 'resist', legislative incursions on values to which they attach much importance. Usually the 'radical' initiative comes from central government seeking to implement measures it has pushed through Parliament but in the **GLC case** it was a local authority trying to use existing statutory powers more fully and aggressively than had previously been the case.

The fact that particular values influence judges in their approach to interpretation is, of course, likely to be more significant where political conflicts lie behind the cases before them. The choices made by judges then become much more noticeable and judgments may well be stigmatised as 'political'. This label will be misleading not because it is inaccurate, but because it implies that this need not be so and that judicial decisions are not normally political.

In fact, the pejorative epithet 'political' is applied
because those affected by the judgment are encouraged by
the rhetoric of the law to believe that the value of
judicial impartiality concerns not only the **process** of
decision-making but also applies to the court's
interpretation of the law. Impartiality, however, is **only**
concerned with the way the law is applied once its meaning
has been established; the ascertainment of its meaning
always involve political choices by both legislators and
judges. The obfuscation of this important distinction is
well exemplified in the Prime Minister's response to the
suggestion that certain aspects of the Court of Appeal's
decision in the **GLC case** was political:

> 'I wholly reject (that). Judges give decisions on the
> law and the evidence before them. They do so totally
> impartially'. [15]

Maintenance of the erroneous belief that impartiality
extends to judicial interpretation of the law is, however,
very important. It is instrumental in maintaining respect
for the law and a willingness to accept the decisions of
the courts. It helps to depoliticise judicial decisions
and the outcome of court cases, enabling it to be suggested
that, if a decision **does** favour some interests as against
others, it does so because that is **the law** which the
courts, having impartially interpreted, are simply required
to apply. Thus, the competing ideologies of judges on the
one hand, and the political policies of a local authority
on the other, can be portrayed as a straight conflict
between those policies and the law.

The ideological interpretations of the law thus have
served to control the policy-making and practices of local
authorities. The interpretations adopted place substantive
limits upon the work of an authority in introducing social
change, in altering the patterns of advantage and power in
their communities.

There was, in some instances a way around the
obstacles. As we have indicated the GLC proved to be
extremely adaptable. Such adaptations were also an
option for Loamshire in respect of its policies to help
black businesses and subsidise the fares of YTS   trainees:

> 'I gave them advice that the Black Busines Scheme would
> be disciminatory and therefore outside the law. They
> did not like this advice. My advice was that if they
> could develop this policy on an area basis so that
> funds were available to particular areas which had a
> high preponderance of blacks then this would be
> accepted legally'. (County Solicitor)

'What I wanted them to do was to implement a marketing
strategy which would lower the fares during off peak
hours thus helping the unemployed yet bringing in
revenue. It is OK to market in this general way that
will indirectly help the unemployed but it is not
acceptable to devise a policy which discriminates
directly in favour of a particular group'. (PTE
Director)

These objectives would, however, only be achieved at a
price that was unacceptable; an accommodation with the law
could only be secured by suppressing any presentation of
the policies as part of the council's radical socialist
philosophy. The GLC's image did not suffer through
adaptation but it may have been politically more
experimental and adept.

Despite this evidence of limited scope for adaptation the
clear function of the law in a period of great social and
political change, interpreted and reinforced by the
judiciary, has been to regulate and control the pace of
change. The judiciary, drawing upon ideologies which
favour private property and traditional notions of
fairness, has reinforced the political arm of the state in
controlling redistribution in favour of local need. The
State and the judiciary have combined to mediate class
interests.

Notes

1. Strictly Rurshire has no place in this matrix as it displayed no response to the **GLC case**, whether on an administrative or a political level. However, its policy preferences on public transport, and on local authority expenditure generally, coincided with or even outstripped the most restrictive interpretation of the implications of the **GLC case**. We have, therefore, given it a notional place in our typology.

2. S. Ranson, B. Hinings and R. Greenwood, 'The Structuring of Organisation Structures', **Administrative Science Quarterly,** March 1980; S. Lukes, **Power: A Radical View,** Macmillan, 1974.

3. O. Lomas, 'Law as a resource and the resourcefulness of law' in S. Ranson, G. W. Jones and K. Walsh (eds), **Between Centre and Locality: The Politics of Public Policy,** Allen & Unwin, 1985.

4. P. McAuslan, **The Ideologies of Planning Law,** Pergamon, 1980.

5. M. Galanter, 'Why the 'Hares' Come out Ahead: Speculations on the Limits of Legal Change', 9 **Law and Society Review** (1974), 95.

6. Lukes, **op. cit.,** P. Saunders, **Urban Politics,** Hutchinson, 1979.

7. Saunders, **op. cit.**

8. P. Bachrach and M. S. Baratz, **Power and Poverty, Theory and Practice,** Oxford University Press, New York, 1970, p. 44.

9. Both barristers.

10. Cf, D. Heald, **Public Expenditure,** Martin Robertson, Oxford, 1983, Ranson, Jones and Walsh, **op. cit.**

11. **R. v. London Transport Executive, ex p. GLC** [1983] 2 All E.R. 262

12. Lomas, **op.cit.**

13. [1955] Ch.210.

14. Lomas, **op. cit.**

15. H.C. Deb., Vol 12, col. 418 (November 10, 1981). We are indebted to C. Harlow and R. Rawlings for bringing this quotation to our attention in their book **Law and Administration**, Weidenfeld & Nicholson, 1984, p. 335, where they discuss the question of "Discretionary Justice?".

9 Summary and conclusion

The tradition of non-litigation began in the 1980s to give way to a more intense period of legal activism. This was highlighted by a number of court cases which focussed upon the policies of metropolitan local authorities to subsidise public transportation: in **Bromley v Greater London Council** together with cases involving a number of the Metropolitan County Councils.

This research has examined the impact these judicial decisions have had on the internal workings and decision-making of those local authorities responsible for public transportation. The study involved interviews in the GLC, three Metropolitan County Councils and two non-Metropolitan (shire) County Councils.

Interviews were arranged with the key members and officers. The interviews explored the history of the Authority's public transport policy; the impact of the May 1981 local elections; the impact of the GLC and related cases on transport policy as well as upon other policy areas and the general effect of judicialisation upon the organisation of local authorities and their decision making processes. Public and private documentation relating to the cases was collected and interpreted.

The research found that the public transport fares cases had implications for the substance of Administrative Law (both for the scope of statutory powers and duties and the exercise of discretionary power) as well as raising more general questions of judicial review in relation to local government. They have also had an effect on the organisation and process of decision-making within local authorities. There were, however, differences in the responses to judicialisation which required both interactionist and structural explanations.

1. Developments in substantive Administrative Law

At the centre of the cases is the nature and extent of the statutory powers of the GLC and the Metropolitan County Councils to subsidise public transport. The judgment that the GLC should adhere to 'ordinary business principles' and avoid treating transport as an 'object of social policy' produced consternation and uncertainty as to the interpretation of their statutory powers. This uncertainty affected the Metropolitan Counties even though the basis of their statutory powers derived from different legislation. Although the court cases in these authorities restored order and certainty to the interpretation of powers in this area, nevertheless, caution in exercising their statutory powers in respect of subsidy remained.

The decisions of the appellate courts implied that the councils had abused their discretionary power. The key underlying principle to emerge is that discretion must be exercised properly and that manifesto commitments or policy decisions are 'relevant considerations' only in decision-making which must always remain open to other relevant considerations such as finance. Likewise, 'fiduciary duty' is now seen not as a separate, but as a relevant consideration when exercising any discretionary power. The judgment of Lord Diplock has been interpreted by senior officers and members of the GLC as making fiduciary duty an overriding obligation on the authority. Although fiduciary duty has had less impact on the Metropolitan Counties, it has nevertheless had a significant cautionary influence on the attitudes of elected members.

2. The general process of judicial review

This was regarded as unsatisfactory by local authority members and officers because of: the uncertainty of the process; the difficulty of proving that legal standards had been observed; and a belief that the adversarial nature of judicial review had a restrictive effect on the legal issues addressed in any given case.

3. The organisation and process of decision-making

The public transport fares cases have had their impact upon the authorities we studied. The research found both common trends and differences between authorities. The trends indicate an association between the experience of judicialisation and the growth in procedure and bureaucracy. The need to demonstrate the reasonableness of decisions has caused authorities to follow procedures ritualistically, prepare lengthier reports, spend more time in meetings: this has, it was argued, made decision-making less efficient. The greater visibility of decision-making is a second trend. This has enhanced public acountability. Yet there is concern that the judicialising of decision-making - with continual reference to counsel and the courts - is creating a technical process that is incompatible with the democratic accountability of elected members.

4. Explanations

Comparative analysis revealed important differences between authorities. Two complied more readily with the legal constraints upon their decision-making. This was explained in the rural county by the process of 'non-decision making' whereby potential challenge as dominant values were thwarted by the mobilisation of bias within the authority. In the Metropolitan County the explanation drew upon a model of 'resource dependency' and the relative distribution of experience, resources and power.

The analysis concluded that these 'interactionist' accounts though providing adequate explanations of the differences between authorities remain incomplete without a more structural analysis to account for emergent trends. Such an analysis identifies, in a period of structural change, the association of State and Judiciary, drawing upon ideologies of private interest and property to regulate the radical plans of local authorities designed to redistribute resources and develop services in relation to local need.

Appendix: the interview schedule

A. **History of authority's public transport policy** - prior to about May 1981

Nature and frequency of debates within the authority

Key issues: main lines of conflict

Did the specific questions of lawfulness of public transport subsidies arise?

Were any outside sources of advice consulted, either by officers or members?

B. **Impact of the May 1981 Local Elections**

Was the subsidisation of public transport a significant issue?

Major party positions on public transport

Key issues: main lines of conflict

Did the specific questions of lawfulness of public transport subsidies arise?

Were any outside sources of advice consulted, either by officers or members?

C.   **Impact of the GLC and related cases**

(if not covered above) When did you first become
aware that your authority's public transport policy
might be subject to legal challenge?

What were the authority's reactions to the
(different stages of the) **GLC case?**

What were felt to be the most significant aspects of
the case?

How was debate initiated within the authority?
Terms of that debate?

Were any specific challenges made/threatened to the
authority's public transport policies at this time?
From whom?

How was any challenge dealt with?   What was the
outcome?

What specific sources of (particularly legal) advice
were sought, both internal and external?

How were they chosen?   Who (officer/member)? What
were they asked?

What did they advise?   How was that advice received?

Were there any conflicts of advice?   How were any
such conflicts handled?

How aware was your authority at this time of what
was happening in other authorities?   How did this
influence your own authority's decision-making?

To what extent were the issues raised by the **GLC
case** unique, or had there been other situations in
the past that you would regard as comparable?

D.   **Impact of the GLC and related cases on other policy
areas**

At what stage did you become aware that the **GLC case**
might have implications in policy areas other than
public transport?

In what areas?   What was the response - in the form
of policies and procedures being changed, advice
being sought etc.?

E. General effects of judicialisation

At what stage of the policy-making process are questions as to the possible lawfulness of particular options/decisions normally considered?

How is this done? Examples?

How is it decided which policies are likely to raise legal problems?

In determining such questions, what is the role played by the authority's own legal adviser? By outside legal advisers? By other sources of advice (e.g. District Auditor, DoE)?

Has the significance of these sources of advice altered since the **GLC** and other related cases?

How are any conflicts of advice resolved?

Can you say how many times and on what issues your authority has in the past year:

(i) sought the opinion of counsel?

(ii) been legally challenged in the courts or by other means over issues of policy (i.e., not including such things as personal injury claims?

(iii) considered or taken legal action itself against some other body on issues of policy?

What are your general views about recent developments regarding issues of legality of local authorities' actions?

Have they influenced procedures in local government? In what ways?